Over the Bluffs

A case of stolen innocence and the ultimate betrayal

by

Lori Parker

Dorrance Publishing Co
585 Alpha Drive
Pittsburgh, PA 15238
Visit our website at www.dorrancebookstore.com

ISBN: 979-8-88925-382-2
eISBN: 979-8-88925-882-7

IN MEMORY OF SUSAN BOX, CAREE COLLISON, AND
NELLIE STANWORTH

Chapter One

When you think of California in the 1960s and 1970s, you think of the hippie movement and how it was all about peace, but it was also an era that saw crimes, and brutal ones at that. We are all aware of the Charles Manson murders in the late 1960s. Times were a little more relaxed back then. Hitchhiking was something that was popular all over the United States, with both men and women. Women were not concerned with their safety at that time. They didn't have social media to keep them informed of the events happening around them. I mean, who really paid attention to the news when you were younger when there was no social media or so many news stations to watch on TV? I didn't grow up in the 60s, but in the 70s we had one TV with rabbit ears.

Pinole, California, was a small but growing town outside of San Francisco during the 60s. Kids would climb over the bluffs to go to Point Wilson and swim in the San Pablo Bay. Kids were just as easy going as everyone else. Today, Pinole is about eighteen minutes from Berkeley, California, but took much longer in the 1960s. As a teenager, if you didn't have transportation, you would have to take a bus or hitchhike to get there.

Unfortunately, the lack of awareness of the evils growing at that time would claim a few victims. Most notably, two young victims who would put Pinole, California, into the spotlight.

Chapter Two

Jane Wallington (pseudonym) was a twenty-year-old nursing student at the local college in Richmond, California. She was just leaving her shift working as a cashier in the men's furnishing department at Montgomery Ward on August 12, 1965, at approximately 5:30 P.M.

When she got into her car, she noticed that it was kind of a warm evening, so she decided to leave the windows down. This would prove to be her undoing.

When she came to a stop sign at Forty-First Street and Bissel, she was approached by a young man on the passenger side of her car. His hair was crew cut, and he was wearing green jeans and a light-colored sport shirt. He looked like an average guy in his early twenties, so she wasn't too alarmed.

While she waited for another car to go through the stop sign, he peeked his head in the open window and asked if she could give him a ride to his car. His car had broken down about a mile down the road and he couldn't find a phone to call for a ride. He looked sincere, but she had always been careful and wasn't comfortable with giving him a ride.

She told him she couldn't because she was in a hurry to get home to study for one of her nursing exams she had the next day. He asked her again, and Jane told him again that she couldn't give him a ride.

After this statement, the look on the guy's face changed; he no longer looked like the average guy. His eyes turned dark, and she could see the anger that came over him. He was not the type of person to take no for an answer. He said something to the effect of "I'm going anyways."

He reached through the passenger side door window, unlocked the door, and got in. As soon as he got in the car, he put a knife to her stomach and told her, "If you scream, I'm going to kill you." He had taken the knife out so fast she didn't have time to react; she was frozen in fear.

He paused for a moment and asked her if she knew where the Berkeley Yacht Club was. Barely able to speak, she told him she did, and he ordered her to "Drive north on Forty-First and Nevin, west on Nevin to 37, and get on the freeway. Then take the Gillman off ramp."

She did as he commanded; she had no other choice. So many things were running through her mind. What if she saw a police car? Could she somehow get their attention without him stabbing her first? What if she just opened the door and jumped out? She couldn't think straight and only did what he ordered her to do. She knew she was in trouble.

When they got off the ramp, she saw the green sign that said Golden Gate Fields, which is a horse track. She relaxed a little, thinking there has to be people here since it was a Thursday. Maybe someone would see her, and she could make her escape. To her disappointment, there was not one car in the parking lot. She knew her fate was sealed.

He demanded she put the car in park and put her hands behind her back so he could tie her up with some sort of electrical wire that was surrounded in plastic.

The guy told her in a casual voice, "I am sorry, but I am going to have to kill you."

Jane was sobbing at this point. She was only twenty years old and was too young to die. She tried to struggle with him when he was forcing her to walk to the south-track parking lot, a place that was secluded and no one could see them. She was a small woman; there was no way she could fight him off, especially with her hands tied. The guy started to unbutton her shirt and pulled it up to her shoulders, exposing her bra. He continued to remove her clothes, all the way to her shoes.

He then started to rape her and choke her. She lost consciousness because she could not breathe. She blacked out and then came to, but she didn't know for how long. He was untying her hands from behind her back and in a calm voice said, "I have finished now. I'm glad I didn't kill you." I believe her fainting was a blessing, so she didn't have to see what was happening to her. I can't imagine feeling helpless and not being able to do anything when you are being raped.

This statement causes you to pause and say, what in the world did he just say? What causes someone to commit an act of violence and then have some sort of conscience to say "I'm glad I didn't kill you," as if he is asking for forgiveness because he didn't kill her.

She didn't know what type of knife he had when he put it against her stomach, but now she saw the knife had a curved blade so it wasn't a normal type of knife that has a straight blade, like a kitchen or steak knife. The man let her get dressed, as if trying to show some sort of respect for her, and told her to get back in the car.

When they got the car, he made her sit on the floorboard of the front passenger seat until they returned to the Montgomery Ward where she worked. He saw her come out of the store beforehand, so he knew she worked there.

During the ride back he said, "I am married with four kids, so I am glad I didn't kill you." He said this so calmly and acted like what he had just done to her never happened.

He went on to state, "I will never do this again."

What sort of man tells a victim, after raping and trying to kill them, their life story?

She was completely numb and didn't care about anything he said. This man looked like the boy next door. Who would think he was a rapist and had a mean streak? Jane certainly didn't when she first saw him, but now she knew better. How would his kids feel if they knew how their father was, and how would his wife feel about it? He just raped her and tried to kill her. It just didn't make sense.

After dropping her off, he took off on foot and she didn't see him again. She went into the store to call the police and report the rape. She had given the police a description of what he looked like, but they were unable to catch him based upon the facts she gave. Of course, telecommunication at the time was not as advanced as today, so it's not too hard to believe they couldn't catch him.

After this assault, she was careful to always have her windows up and doors locked whenever she was in the car. She wasn't going to let that happen again.

Chapter Three

On November 4, 1965, Emily Duncan (pseudonym), twenty-four years old, was walking home from doing some Christmas shopping at the shopping center in El Sobrante, California, outside the Richmond, California, area.

It was around 8:30 P.M., so the sun had already gone down a few hours earlier. It was getting a little chilly out, around 55 degrees. The breeze off the Bay always made it a bit cooler. She was walking home near the San Pablo housing project, just enjoying the night after a day of shopping. The hills of California in the evening could be very calming when you are surrounded by quiet. The way the houses were scattered was like the favelas in Brazil, house upon house right on up the hill, stacked right on top of each other the closer you get to the city. Emily could only think of the nice day she had and did not think about any dangers that may be awaiting her on her way home. On this night, there was a danger she could not have imagined.

As Emily was walking by an open field that was on her left, a man jumped out of nowhere from her right and snatched her, holding a curved knife to her throat. She was taken by surprise and frozen in fear. She could not see his face; she only heard his voice.

He whispered in her ear, "You need to do what I tell you, or I will have to kill you."

She struggled as much as she could to try and get away without him digging the knife into her throat, but it was no use. If she struggled too much, he would end up cutting her, and most certainly kill her.

She took a quick glance at her surroundings and knew there was nowhere to run, and this was just a walking path; no one was going to be walking that at night. She had no other choice but to give up and comply. What was going through her mind: Was he going to rape her, kill her, or both? She can survive being raped, but she had four kids; she couldn't let him kill her. As he was dragging her into the field, she was pleading with him.

"Please don't kill me. I have four kids that need me. You don't need to do this. If you let me go, I won't tell anyone." It appeared he didn't even hear her because he just kept dragging her, ignoring her pleas.

When he got her where he wanted her, he proceeded to bind her wrists with an insulated wire that he had with him. She wasn't sure where he got it from because she didn't see it in his hand when he grabbed her and dragged her into the field. Most likely it had to have come from his pocket. This was the same type of wire that was used on Jane Wallington, which was realized later in the investigation.

It was cloudy that evening, so the moon was not shining, which provided the darkness he needed to do what he set out to do. Even though it was dark, he caught a glimpse of her face and saw the fear on her face, which only made him more excited as he was about to rape her. That was what he enjoyed, seeing the fear in their eyes and on their faces. Making them feel lesser of a person, he was the superior one. Binding her wrists made it all the more pleasurable because he was in complete control. He could do whatever he wanted and that was powerful to him. *No woman is going to boss me around anymore,* was his mentality at that moment.

After hearing her continuous pleas, something in him changed. Instead of raping her, he decided to just rob her of $15 (which is roughly $121 today). Maybe her pleading that she had four kids and not to kill her changed his mind. After all, he had kids of his own.

Before leaving her, he told her, "I know where you live. I looked at your driver's license and you never know when I am going to pay you a visit. Always remember that," and he ran off into the night.

Emily ran to her friend's house that lived not far from there, who persuaded her to call the police. She was very reluctant to do so since he warned her that he knew where she lived, but she relented, for her kids' sake.

Reporting it to the police didn't subside the fear she still had. After this day, she didn't let her kids out of her sight for very long, and would constantly look over her shoulder, always wondering when he would be back.

Chapter Four

On May 13, 1966, Pamela Scott (pseudonym) was twenty years old and living in Richmond, California. On this night, around 9:00 P.M., she had pulled into the parking lot of Richmond High School next to the auto shop. They were having a dance at the school, and she was going to see if she could find one of her friends that she went to high school with. Her friend was two years younger and ready to graduate. She was talking to a gentleman at the door by the name of Steve, who stated she could not go in because she was no longer a student attending that high school. She tried to talk her way in, but he wouldn't budge and she had no other choice but to leave. Since they didn't have cell phones during those times, she couldn't call or text to let her friend know she wasn't allowed in.

She pulled up to a stop sign coming out of the school parking lot when she saw this guy walking up to her car. He looked older but was clean cut and didn't look like a danger to her. Her doors weren't locked, so the man opened the door on the passenger's side and jumped in. He was so quick she had no time to react. He put a knife against her abdomen and said, "If you do what I tell you, I won't kill you. Just do as I say."

She was only twenty years old. What was she supposed to do? She was paralyzed with fear for a few seconds until she realized what was happening.

It was dark out so he could pretty much get away with whatever he wanted. He didn't say anything until they were on a residential street and ordered her to stop in front of one of the houses that had a white picket fence in the front.

He told her, "Now I'm going to drive."

As she was going to get out of the car to go around to the passenger side, he grabbed her by the hair and dragged her back into the car.

"Don't do that again!" he yelled. His voice had changed and was deeper than it was when he got in the car, so she knew he was mad. He bound her hands behind her back using an electrical wire that had one red wire and one white wire and pushed her on the passenger side floorboard. He drove to Point Richmond, which was about five to ten miles away.

Once they came to a stop, he dragged Pamela out of the car and threw her to the ground. He then started slapping her in the face and attempting to remove her top. Pamela's face was stinging from when he slapped her, but he didn't care. She knew that she needed to do as he asked, or it could become much worse than him slapping her around.

He couldn't get her blouse over her head because her hands were bound, so he asked her, "If I untie your hands, will you promise not to try anything?"

Pamela had no other options, so she told him, "No, I won't run."

During the ride to where he was taking her, she was looking for a way to escape. He only bound her wrists; maybe when he opens the door, she could run for it. But would there be anyone around to help her?

When they reached Point Richmond, which overlooked the San Francisco Bay, she knew it wasn't going to matter if she ran; he was too quick for her and there was no one around to help her. He knew no one would be out there at that time of night to interfere with what he had planned.

Once he parked the car, he grabbed her off the floorboard by knife point and demanded, "Go down to the beach and take off your clothes."

As she stumbled down to beach, she was looking around hoping to see lights of any kind to indicate there were other people around but saw nothing. She felt defeated. She just gave up at that point.

He went on to tell her, "I'll untie your hands if you promise to be good and not try anything."

"I promise," she said in between sobs.

His previous crimes were of rape and threatening to kill his victims, but this one was different. He decided to do something different. Maybe if he did, the police wouldn't think he was a suspect in this crime. After fondling her for a while, he decided he wanted oral sex instead of raping her. She was twenty years old, and this man seemed a little bit older than her.

He proceeded to pull out his penis and force her to give him oral sex. She had never done this before, so she initially choked as he forced her mouth down. She gagged and pulled back and he slapped her in the face.

"Don't do that again or I will give you more than a slap," he commanded.

She needed to compose herself before he became really angry and did something worse. He forced her mouth down onto his penis again until he was satisfied. She felt so disgusted that she almost threw up, and at this point was angry at herself. How could this man do this to her? How could she put herself in this situation?

When he was finished, he demanded, "You are not getting your clothing back. Walk to the car."

At some point he must have felt some sort of remorse because he gave her back her clothes. It makes you wonder if he did things differently this time because he didn't want to get caught or because she was so young?

He drove the same route back to the high school that they had taken to the Point. He just raped her and then decided to take her back to the high school where someone could see him and identify him. If he didn't want to be caught, he sure wasn't avoiding it.

Before getting out of her car he told her, "I'm going to come back for you if you ever tell the authorities. I will find you and follow you home to find out where you live, and I will get you then. You never know when I'm going to show up."

From then on Pamela would make sure she was never alone outside of her house. She would always have someone walk her to her car and her doors were always locked. I would imagine this tore apart her sense of security and made her very cautious and untrusting of others, not to mention issues with personal rela-tionships.

Chapter Five

Susan Box was fifteen years old and living in Pinole, California, in 1966. Pinole is about twenty to thirty minutes from San Francisco over the Oakland Bay Bridge. Susan was very thin with brown eyes and shoulder-length blondish-brown hair. She and her family had moved to Pinole in 1963 from Dover, England.

The Boxes were involved with the Salvation Army, which is how they came to the United States. At the time, you had to have a sponsor to move to the United States from another country. A minister and his family volunteered to be their sponsor. They came to the United States so "Len" (Leonard), Susan's father, could find a better job. Len worked at the Mechanic's Bank in Richmond while her mother, Peggie, worked for the Salvation Army offices in San Francisco.

Susan had a younger sister, Verena, and an older sister, Carol. The Boxes lived in a modest home in Pinole and would walk just about everywhere. Pinole was growing, but the main cities were Richmond and Berkeley. The bus was the main form of transportation for those who didn't have a car or who chose not to drive from Pinole. Susan and her sisters were familiar with this mode of transportation as well, but the bus stop was quite a distance from their house. There were many times the girls would just hitchhike, which was very common in 1966. These kids seemed to have no fear of hitchhiking or public transportation.

The love of Susan's life was animals. She loved working with horses and her dog, which was a Samoyed named Nikky. If you saw Susan, you saw Nikky.

Susan was very talented in that she sewed her own clothes. I would imagine with three girls it wouldn't have been cheap for the Boxes to provide for all of them.

It was said Susan was loved by the neighbors. They all said she had a love of toddlers who loved her British accent. Who in America doesn't like a British accent? She spent a lot of time doing things with the Salvation Army. She was in the choir and sometimes played the cymbals and tambourine.

But Susan was unhappy about living in the United States and wanted to return to England, even though her sister and parents enjoyed living here. One day Susan's older sister said to her, while watching the Super Bowl, that she would move back to England if Susan did. Obviously Susan wasn't the only one who was completely unhappy living in the United States.

The girls had made friends while in the Salvation Army, but it was not an easy transition. Although, I do believe the culture then would have been more accepting of them than they are now.

She would babysit regularly for a couple, the Eddy's, who had three young children and lived about a mile and a half down the road. If Susan's dad couldn't take her over there, she would just walk. It would take roughly thirty to forty minutes to get there by walking. Susan lived on Tennant Avenue in Pinole and the Eddy's lived on Alamo Drive. Along the walk to the Eddy's, Susan would stop at the Short Stop Restaurant to grab a bite to eat. The owners, the Polries, were always friendly to her and said hello whenever she came. Sometimes Susan would have her close friend Caree with her, so they knew both girls.

Susan, along with many other girls her age, was obsessed with the Beatles. In 1964, the Beatles had come to the United States for one of their first concerts. They performed at the Cow Palace in Daly City, California, southwest of San Francisco. Susan and her older sister Carol got wind of the name of the hotel the Beatles were going to be staying at and camped out trying to see them in person. Unfortunately, that didn't pan out and they didn't get to see them. I can imagine the excitement they had; after all the Beatles were from their own country.

Chapter Six

Susan's best friend, Caree Collison, was also Susan's age. Both were sophomores at De Anza High School. Some said they were like twins except for their hair. Caree had long black hair and Susan had blondish-brown hair. In junior high, Caree participated in GAA, which was the Girls Athletic Association. She had participated in all kinds of different sports such as gymnastics, running, and archery. Although Caree was very slender, she was pretty strong from doing various sports. My mother was in the same club and remembers Caree as being timid and quiet.

Caree was the only child to Larry and her stepmom, Emily Collison. Caree's biological mother, Flora May Croze, died from polio when Caree was a toddler. Larry and Caree's mom were only married for three years before she passed. As you will read, it is very unfortunate for Caree that she lost her biological mother; it would have changed the sequence of events that Caree will have to endure.

Larry Collison met and married Emily Shamanski when Caree was around three years old. According to a member of the Collison family, Emily was not mother material. She didn't want Caree at the wedding or reception when they got married. Larry saw this as a warning sign about how she would be as a stepmom, but he went through with the wedding anyway. Caree needed a mother in her life. Her stepmother did not want her around and her father, Larry, did not support Caree in the aspect of putting his only child first.

Caree spent a majority of her time with her uncle Vernon and aunt Jimmie in Concord, California, which is about thirty to forty minutes away. She loved spending time with her cousins. It is very heartbreaking to hear of the way she had been forgotten about by her own father, the only parent she had left and should be able to depend on. Caree was his daughter, and he should have told Emily that Caree should be staying with him, not his brother Vernon.

Caree wrote poetry and was a good student. Her favorite quote is from Shakespeare: *"You know it's possible, Octavian, that when you die you will die without ever having been alive."*

This quote, unfortunately, was the way of Caree's life. She did not know what it was to be alive, and be loved, except for the love of her aunt, uncle and cousins. I am sure her father loved her, but he certainly didn't put her interests above his own or his wife's. For example, right before the end of the school year Caree had written a letter to her father stating her uncle said she was going to be with her dad but Larry was going to Canada. So she asks him "where am I supposed to go"? I just can't imagine the pain she must have felt by what her father was doing to her.

According to a Collison family member, on Friday, July 29, 1966, Caree was having lunch with her father when she asked him when she could come home. At that point Larry decided enough was enough and he was going to go home and tell Emily that if she couldn't accept Caree then their marriage would not work out. He told Caree he wanted her to come home on Monday, after the weekend. According to other sources, Larry stated at that time that his brother, Vernon, was going to pick up Caree at 5:00 P.M. on Monday when he got out of work. So, I'm not so sure he planned on taking a stand against Emily when it came to Caree. Caree's father was the principal at Dover Elementary School in El Sobrante, California. For someone who works around kids, you would think he would try to have a relationship with his only daughter.

According to this same family member, the events that actually occurred on Monday, August 1, 1966, were that Caree's uncle Vernon dropped her off at her own house instead of Susan's. Emily did not allow Caree to have a key to the house. When her uncle dropped her off at her house with her belongings, she tried to get into the house, but both of her parents were gone and the doors were locked. She had no other choice but to walk to Susan's. Susan was about a thirty-to forty-five-minute walk from her house.

Other sources state that her uncle did in fact drop Caree off at Susan's house, not her own house, on his way to work in San Francisco.

Caree was looking forward to seeing Susan; they always had fun together. When Caree arrived, Susan came out of the house to greet her. Susan had a babysitting job at the Eddy's later in the day so the girls thought they would just hang out in Berkeley until then.

Before taking off, Susan told her mom that they were going to go out and then head over to the Eddy's to babysit, not mentioning anything about going to Berkeley.

At the time, Berkeley was the place to go for teenagers and young adults. Berkeley was a college town, home to the University of California Berkeley. It was also known as hippie central. This is where the hippies went during those days. Susan was a very carefree person so she would have fit right in. Traveling to Berkeley took some time in the sixties. Susan and Caree would have to walk fifteen to twenty minutes to the bus stop and then another thirty-five- to forty-five-minute bus ride to get there.

The thing that bothers me, or that I can't pinpoint, is there are many sources that say they were going to Berkeley, but I can't figure out why. What would make two teenage girls want to go to Berkeley on a Monday morning in August? I have tried to locate events that happened that day, but there was nothing at Berkeley. One source states Susan was to babysit that morning. A friend of the family stated that if Susan needed to babysit at the Eddy's her father, Len, would just drive her over there.

There are a couple different versions of what happened next. According to a Collison family member, Larry was told the girls were waiting for a bus, but other versions state the girls were hitchhiking, which was common practice. I will have to go with the hitchhiking, which seems to be the overall consensus of what the girls were doing.

Since they often ate at the Short Stop Restaurant down the street from where Susan lived, they were familiar with the driver of a van that was passing by as being the fry cook at the restaurant.

All that is left of this restaurant today is a small building with boarded-up windows. You would have no idea this was a restaurant because of how small it is. It is the size of a small house. You can see the vent on the top of the building, which is the only indication it was a former restaurant. I wish I had been able to see inside to get a better idea of the layout and how it could even be a restaurant with how small it was.

The guy passed by them, stopped, and put it in reverse to pick them up. It was stated by one witness that the girls "were standing on the corner displaying their legs, carrying on as teenagers do in a mildly sexually provocative fashion." On this particular day, it was reported the girls were wearing a gray sweater, blue denim trousers, a light brown suede jacket, and a gold and blue jersey. It is uncertain who wore what that day. Regardless of how they were dressed or acting, they were teenage girls, innocent and naïve to some extent. Their age should have made a difference when it comes to doing the right thing or the wrong thing, but it did not matter on this day.

When the driver of the van backed up to the girls, he rolled down the window and asked them where they were going. Susan told them they were headed for Berkeley to hang out before their babysitting job. He proceeded to tell them he was going that way and could give them a ride. Since they in essence knew him, they didn't seem to be afraid.

The girls looked at each other and the answer from each one was told from their eyes when they looked at one another. They decided what they heck, they might as well. He didn't seem like a threat.

Unfortunately, he had no intention of taking them to Berkeley. His intent was something more sinister, and he made that decision when he saw them on the road hitchhiking.

Chapter Seven

It was about 8:00 A.M. when Dennis Stanworth came across the girls standing in front of the gas station hitchhiking. He had recognized the blonde girl, not only from the Short Stop restaurant where he worked but he had also seen her a few times babysitting for his neighbor's kids, the Eddy's. They only lived three doors down from him. Dennis had just moved to the neighborhood, so the Eddy's only saw him a few times but stated they seemed like a nice family. He also recognized the black-haired girl from the Short Stop Restaurant. The girls would come in together at times.

As he was passing by the girls, something came over him. He stated that a rage came over him. "I saw them there and I thought, 'You dirty lousy bitches. I'm going to kill you.'" Keep in mind that these were two fifteen-year- old girls. The anger he felt toward them was an issue he had from his past. He stated, "I hated them, I hated what they'd done to me." So, what had women done to him? Ignored him and threw him aside? And what causes a man to be angry with two young teenage girls who were innocent and had nothing to do with his past or his anger toward women?

As the girls got into the panel van, he was telling himself, "You don't want to do this," but he didn't have control over his life at that point; he felt he had to do it. He had a stolen gun under the seat and that was going to be what he would use on them to make them obey.

The girls were just chatting among themselves in the van when they noticed he wasn't driving the right way toward Berkeley.

The girls became a little concerned, so Caree asked where they were going because they weren't taking the right way to Berkeley. He stated he needed to stop at the lumber store real quick and then they would go.

He still didn't seem like a threat during this time. They were a little concerned and uncomfortable, but what were they going to do? They were already in the van, and it seemed like a plausible explanation.

Instead of going to the lumberyard, he drove them to Point Wilson, which overlooks the San Pablo Bay. When he stopped, the girls were confused, and that is when he grabbed the gun underneath his seat and pointed it at them. The girls couldn't believe what was happening. They knew him. Why would he do this?

He ordered them to "Start walking up to the bluffs or I'll kill you right here."

As they were approaching the bluffs, he could see some brush that would cover them as he was about to satisfy his rage. The girls were crying and asking him why he was doing this to them.

Dennis just ignored them and kept marching them up the hill. I can't imagine the fear the girls felt at this time.

Caree was trying to think of a way to escape. There was a lot of brush. Maybe if they ran he wouldn't be able to catch them. After all, Caree was in sports and had experience in running long distances. When they got over the bluffs, he saw thick brush and decided to hide in there so no one would see them.

Once they got there he ordered them to "Take your clothes off, now."

Caree decided this was their time to escape. She yelled at Susan and told her, "Susan, go around the brush and run, as fast as you can." Dennis was too quick and was able to grab Susan before she could run away. Caree had already gained some distance, but didn't make it far enough, and Susan wasn't able to escape at all. He looked at Caree and yelled, "If you don't get back here right now, I will shoot and kill your friend. Come back right now."

To be put in this situation of having to make a choice between self-preservation and helping her friend could not have been easy for Caree, but she did as she was told because she loved her friend. When she reluctantly came back, he shot her twice in the head and she fell to the ground, motionless.

Susan screamed and asked Dennis if he had killed her friend, to which he replied, "I guess so." He told her to keep disrobing, or he was going to shoot her too.

Susan, being courageous and defiant, said, "If my friend is dead, then go ahead and shoot me." She was not going to let him see her as weak and scared. At this point, she was mad more than she was scared because he had killed her best friend. She stood up to him but, unfortunately, he did what she said to do; he shot her in the head as well.

Dennis stated that he was scared and the gun "just went off." Susan fell to the ground and for some unknown reason, other than being sick and demented, Dennis decided to rape her. I couldn't imagine being shot in the head and then have to sit there waiting to die, if she hadn't died already, while being raped at the same time. The only thing we could hope for was that she died instantly.

Caree, on the other hand, did not succumb to her injuries right then. She may have had to endure the sounds of what was happening to her friend. Both girls were victims to Dennis's obsessions and need for control. They did nothing to ask for this, other than innocently ask for a ride.

The last sounds and smells were of San Pablo Bay, the smell of salt from the ocean, and the slight breeze that comes off the water. I can't imagine what was going through these girls' minds, other than pure fear and anger. Anger from Susan because he shot her friend, and Caree would have been in turmoil, emotionally, of having to save herself or trying to save her friend.

After Dennis was finished, he covered them up with some brush so they would not be seen. He did not think either girl was alive but as he was leaving, he heard one of the girls moan. One of them was still alive. Dennis was scared at this point and just turned around and put a few shots into the bush and left them there.

Dennis felt no remorse afterward. He got back in his van and drove off. When asked how Dennis felt after killing Susan, he stated "rage." He stated, "She wasn't real. It was all in my head. They were just symbols. If they would have been real, it never would have happened." What kind of symbols were they to Dennis?

How do you determine whom to look at like symbols and ones that are human beings? He obviously knew what he was doing; there should be no question of whether or not he was insane. He could have kept going instead of stopping to pick them up, but he gave in to the temptations and hatred he had toward women. He also methodically covered up the girls so they couldn't be found; that sounds like someone who knows exactly what they are doing.

Chapter Eight

After the girls failed to arrive at the Eddy's, Susan's parents contacted Caree's parents a few times that day asking if they had heard anything. When Susan's mom called Larry again at 11:00 that night, she asked Larry if he had heard from the girls because they had not.

Larry stated that he hadn't heard anything either, so he was going to start driving around and see if he could find them. He said he would update her if he happened to find anything. It was a very, very long night for both families.

At that time, the population of Pinole was somewhere around 6,100 people. Even with this small-sized town, Larry had no luck in finding them. He and Susan's parents decided to wait to call the police, thinking the girls would be home any minute. After all, they were teenage girls and could be unpredictable. The next morning when the girls failed to come home, they called the police and reported the girls missing.

This must have been nerve wrecking for these parents, not knowing where their kids were. With no cell phones back then, you were just left to your own devices to think of all the bad things that could be happening to your child and there was nothing you could do. They could only pray they were safe and would eventually come home, but that was not to be.

Police went out to find any type of clue and question people on whether or not they had seen the girls. One witness who was at the gas station stated he had seen them that Tuesday morning around 8:00 am getting into a car. According to the coroner's report of time of death for Susan, the girls had been missing since Monday, so this is not an accurate statement.

Chapter Nine

On August 3, 1966, around 1:30 P.M., three teenage boys, who were best friends, had gone to Point Wilson to go swimming. As they were walking home on the railroad tracks, they heard a moan coming from some brush. The boys didn't know what to think of it, so they pulled the branches back and there were two girls, one lying motionless and the other one moaning and non-responsive.

The boys ran up the hill to the houses and started banging on a couple of doors until someone opened. They called the police and told them what they found. The boys were shaken and scared to death. According to one of the boys, the police officer first on the scene, Deputy Sheriff Douglas Young, started grilling the boys as if they were the ones who did it. They were just walking home and had no idea what happened. After additional questions and listening to the boys, Sheriff Young believed their version of events and let them go. Fearful the killer was still out there, one of the boys stated that he went into hiding from the media, believing they may be next.

The moaning the boys heard in the brush was from Caree. She had not succumbed to her injuries at that point. This strong girl would hold on for another forty-two days before joining her friend. Susan had already passed, and we can only hope that she felt no pain, and just felt the love of Jesus Christ wrapping his arms around her and welcoming her home until her friend could join her.

The girls were left lying next to each other. They had sustained more gunshot wounds when Dennis had turned around and shot through the brush.

According to Caree's autopsy report, she had an additional gunshot wound to the left middle finger. Susan had an additional gunshot wound to the right leg. Both girls had numerous scrapes and bruises, which indicated these two girls tried to put up a fight, but you have no chance when you're up against a gun. The girls were found partially nude. Susan's bra and panties were partly torn from her body and Caree was nude except for her panties. The witness's statement of the girls said the girls were "standing on the corner, displaying their legs, carrying on as teenagers do in a mildly sexually provocative fashion," which is absurd. How can a teenager in a sweater or jersey with jeans be "provocative"? The clothes teenagers wear nowadays can be considered that but jeans and a top? They had no skin showing.

I cannot fathom this way of thinking from a male. But, after reading numerous articles about how women were described back then, they were only looked at like a piece of meat, in my opinion. A lot of times the news media would use "pretty girl" or "pretty woman." I believe that mentality is worse in current times due to social media and news outlets. My mom always said they don't leave anything to the imagination with what some girls wear.

Chapter Ten

During the time the girls were missing, the Box family went into hiding. Susan's parents, Len and Peggie, stayed with their pastor, and the girls stayed with a family friend due to the media camping out in front of their house. They had enough to deal with. Being bombarded with cameras and questions was not something they could handle at the time. They were a very close and quiet family and did not put their "business out for the world to see," as things are today with social media.

Caree's family, on the other hand, stayed in their home and her father had spoken with the media a few times. Caree's father made the statement he could see Point Wilson from his living room window, where the girls lay for two days. When I went to their house, I am not sure how that was possible due to the hills and trees between his home and Point Wilson, but I cannot find what it looked like back then, so I suppose it's possible.

During the time they were missing, Susan's mother, Peggie, was riding back and forth to San Francisco each day for work with a family friend. On that Wednesday, August 3, 1966, on her way home from work, Susan's mom heard the announcement on the radio that two girls were found in Pinole, one of them dead. It was probably a good thing the friend was driving when she heard this. Can you imagine the silence in the car? And what do you say, even if you know that most likely it was Susan and Caree? As a mother, I can't imagine the pain Susan's mother felt, but maybe at the same time, deep down inside she had a sense of hope that it wouldn't be the girls. That had to be the longest drive of her life and in the end, her hope (if she had any) was taken away. The Boxes' daughter had been murdered. I am not sure if the authorities had divulged to them at the time that she had also been raped.

When Larry heard the news on the radio that two girls had been found shot near Pinole, he had called the sheriff's office to see if it was the girls that they found and was told they didn't think it was. He then received a knock on his door around 5:30 P.M. and was told of Caree being shot and in a coma at the hospital and that her friend Susan was dead.

As a parent, I am sure he felt relieved and at the same time heartbroken for Susan's family. The girls were outside in the elements for two days. The weather during that time was mild, in the mid-sixties, but very chilly at night. Caree was alive for those two days and it makes you wonder if she felt anything. Did she feel the breeze off the bay? Was she cold? Was she brain dead and didn't feel anything? It is hard to say; you can only pray that she had no idea what was going on.

When it came time to identify Susan's body, according to a member of the Box family, a family friend had to identify Susan because her father, Len, couldn't bring himself to do it. The most heartbreaking thing is Susan hadn't been cleaned up for identification. When the coroner arrived that day around 6:00 P.M., he described her appearance as having a large amount of dried blood in her hair on the right side of her head, and blood was smeared across her forehead and on her cheek. This family friend says he remembers that day like it was yesterday. That image is not something you could easily get out of your mind. This precious fifteen-year-old being seen the way she was, decomposing and bloodied, and knowing what happened to her just breaks my heart. She deserved more respect than that, but maybe that's the way things were back then.

According to the autopsy report on Susan, she had numerous abrasions and puncture wounds about her body. There was a small caliber bullet in the small intestines, which was removed and given to the criminologist, John Thornton. The report states, "A sagittal fracture of the cranium exists. A bullet has passed through the brain, entering the brain over the medial aspect of the superior portion of the right frontal lobe and then proceeding and to the left, coming to rest at a point on the undersurface of the left occipital lobe." In layman's terms, she was shot on the right side of the forehead. They noted that the bullet they removed was quite fragmented. She had also sustained a bullet wound to her right leg, which was through and through. I would also speculate that this was sustained when Dennis turned around and shot through the brush as he was leaving. Sadly they did find semen inside her. He obviously was excited by what he was doing while he was raping her. I can't imagine her surviving and possibly being impregnated by this monster. It's a question often asked in the world today when it comes to abortion: Should it be allowed under these circumstances?

The official cause of death was brain damage due to a gunshot wound to the head. Whether or not Susan died instantly will be brought into question in the future, in a very sickening sense.

Susan's memorial was held on August 8, 1966, at the Salvation Army Citadel in Oakland, California.

Her Sunday school teacher, Kenneth Hill, delivered her eulogy. He stated, "The world has been a richer place for her presence."

Her funeral was also attended by Caree's parents, and a number of teenage friends from school. Brigadier Kenneth Anderson stated the family didn't want any hatred directed toward anyone involved with the tragedy, and that says a lot about her family and faith. I would have a hard time putting away my anger if someone did that to my child.

A letter written from Susan to a friend the Sunday before her murder stated, "I have found again my faith in God, I hope you will too." I find this very comforting knowing that she found God again and was comforted by him in her last minutes. Two hymns were sung, "Around the Throne" (which was Susan's favorite), and "I'm In His Hands." Susan's final resting place is in the Oakmont Cemetery in Lafayette, California.

Chapter Eleven

Caree was admitted to Brookside Hospital in Richmond and made it through a three-hour surgery to remove the bullet fragments from her brain. She had remained unconscious since she was found. It wasn't until 8:30 that evening when her dad was finally able to see her. At the hospital there was an officer outside her door twenty-four hours a day, only allowing doctors and nurses on the floor, not knowing whether the assailant would come back and finish her off.

For three days, she held her own but started to deteriorate on August 7 and had to be put on a respirator. Shortly after her admission, her kidneys started to fail, and she would no longer respond to the aid of machines or medicine. Brookside didn't have the capability to keep Caree alive with what they had at their disposal, so they moved her to Moffitt Hospital (now named University of California Medical Center in San Francisco) to take advantage of their artificial kidney machine. She had also developed a staph infection while at Brookside. She had shown some improvement at one point to where she could move her hands and would make sounds, so they felt that was encouraging.

Police held onto hope that Caree would regain consciousness to tell them what happened, but she never did and passed away quietly around 4:00 A.M. on September 12, 1966. She was one strong girl to hold on that long. I can only hope that she was dreaming, didn't feel any pain, and just peacefully made her way home to the Lord and her best friend. She would be loved more in heaven than she was on earth.

Since her dad was the principal of Dover Elementary, the Dover Teachers Association set up the Caree Collison Fund to help Caree's dad pay for medical bills and funeral expenses. By December 1966, it had grown to $2,600, which would be around $20,000 today. The Dover School PTA also set up a scholarship fund, which was a total of $777 at that time.

According to Caree's autopsy report, the official cause of death was acute bronchopneumonia due to lacerations of the brain due to a gunshot wound to the head. The diagnosis also adds renal tubular necrosis, which is lack of oxygen and blood flow to the kidneys, causing kidney failure. The coroner described her as "wasted appearing." Her skull was open with three "burr-hole-type incisions" over the right temple. A bullet was found in the midline of the small space in the skull found near the brainstem and the cerebellum part of the brain. Caree had also sustained a gunshot wound to her left middle finger. She could have sustained that when Dennis was going to shoot her, and she put her hand up to deflect the bullet or sustained it when Dennis shot back into the brush when he heard her moan. There was also a metallic fragment in her stomach.

A service was held for Caree on September 15, 1966, at 11:15 A.M., at the Civic Center Chapel of the Wilson & Kratzer Mortuaries. Her service was conducted by the Reverend Palmer Watson of the MacArthur Community Baptist Church. She was laid to rest in the Rolling Hills Memorial Park in Richmond, California. The Collison family wanted anyone donating to send money to the Kidney Foundation in Caree's honor.

Chapter Twelve

Dennis Stanworth was a twenty-four-year-old painter and part time fry cook who lived in Pinole, California, in 1966. He moved to a fairly new house at 2406 Alamo Street around May 1966. The house was quite small for a family of six, but it was his and he was proud of that. Dennis was married with four kids, two of which were his biological children with his current wife, Pamela. Dennis and Pamela had married in 1962. As a hobby, Dennis had been working on the twin hulls of a catamaran that he was building, and reportedly planning on having the hulls airlifted to the Bay so he could "sail his family around the world." Dennis was very talented in the field of carpentry.

He identified as a Mormon but did not actively practice as an adult. According to Bishop N. L. Allphin, Dennis was ordained as a deacon at the age of twelve and then as a teacher of the Mormon faith when he was fourteen. I spoke with a friend of mine, who is Mormon, who stated that at the age of sixteen they would automatically be ordained as a priest. Dennis didn't have this title, so it was obvious he did not continue with the Mormon covenants after being ordained as a teacher.

He grew up with his biological parents, Nellie and Thirl (who went by Stan), and two younger brothers, Larry and Paul. Larry was ten years younger than Dennis, and Paul was only two years younger. Paul stated that he looked up to Dennis and would try to do the same things he did, but that neither one of them had gotten along with their father, although family members did not witness any sort of animosity or anger between Stan and the boys. The boys were young—they may have had just the usual disagreements or arguments between kids and their parents—but nothing to explain why Dennis became the way he was.

Stan and Nellie married on July 11, 1940. Stan joined the military in 1943, when Dennis was six months old. It was in the military that Thirl received the nickname "Stan." According to a family member, he was given this nickname because his superiors had a hard time with his first name, Thirl. Stan excelled in the military. During basic training, it was reported he had received five medals for bayonetting, rifleman, Browning automatic rifle gunner, hand grenades, and marksmanship. He served with the First Army, who were the ones that landed first in France on D-Day and had survived. He had been wounded a couple of times and then sent right back to the field and he had the scar to prove it on his back shoulder from shrapnel. I am sure that he not only had physical scars, but also emotional scars. It could not have been easy to see what he had seen and experienced. According to a family member, he had received a purple heart. I couldn't find his name in the Purple Heart database, but that very well may be because no one enrolled him. He was finally able to come home in 1945. On Thanksgiving Day, he had called his parents and Nellie to let them know he was in New York and would be home that week. He never openly spoke about his military experiences with family, but family members can remember his laugh, which was "big and contagious."

In regard to Dennis, Nellie described him as a good boy but "he was the type of person who needed to be babied all the time." Others described him as a "model youth." Dennis would later state that his mom would call him her "darling daughter" since he was basically a mama's boy and would stay in the house helping her.

Dennis stated he felt alone when he was younger and was without any friends during his teenage years. His father was a hard worker and felt that if you work hard and not show your feelings, you would be fine. The only reference I find regarding any friends of Dennis was the Benwoods, a couple that owned the drive-in Dennis would frequent when he was sixteen years old. The other set of friends that is mentioned is during the sixties when he lived in Pinole, was the Willis and the Polries.

Dennis had a history of attempting to commit suicide. His first suicide attempt was taking a bunch of his mother's migraine pills. He stated, "I just knew that things weren't right, and I didn't feel anybody cared." His good friend, Bill Benwood, would give him the key to his restaurant, and allowed him to sleep there a few times. One morning Mr. Benwood came to the restaurant and found Dennis. Mr. Benwood decided to call Dennis's father to come and pick him up. I would imagine his father was confused on how Dennis was feeling or why he did it, and probably angry that he had embarrassed him like that. He wouldn't want people to know that his own son tried to commit suicide. That was a subject that was not discussed.

What Dennis considered as a suicide attempt was when he was married and decided to purchase a motorcycle. He would drive recklessly, not caring if he died. I wouldn't necessarily say this was a suicide attempt; it's more like lacking the will to live. I doubt anyone knew or caught on to Dennis's lack of caring for his own life, and if they had their suspicions, they did nothing about it.

You never want someone to die of his or her own accord, but had he achieved the goal he may have saved a lot of people a lot of pain in the future. So, how do you justify when it is and is not okay for someone to take his or her own life? This was obviously a cry for help, but during this time mental illness was not accepted or widely discussed. So, Dennis dealt with his issues by working hard. Would getting help be of any benefit to him? In the future it seems to help at some point, but not when it was absolutely necessary.

Dennis felt confused and questioned his own feelings about things. You hear often that those who are cruel to animals have the potential to kill a human being. In Dennis's case he had seen a TV show where someone had killed a dog because they were crazy. In his mind he thought, *Should I kill an animal to see if I'm crazy?* So, that is what he decided to do, but he killed a cat instead of a dog. He stated he couldn't decide either way whether he was crazy after doing this. On the outside looking in, that is a major point when it comes to describing how someone becomes a killer. If you are able to kill a vulnerable animal just out of spite or meanness, then most times you are certainly capable of killing a vulnerable human being. Everyone has the capability to murder; it is a matter of whether or not you succumb to the reasons of right and wrong.

Dennis was certainly nothing like his father. He had joined the Army in 1960 but ended up going AWOL. He felt alone and when they wouldn't give him the job of cryptology he decided to say "the hell with it." The Army discharged him as general discharge under honorable conditions, with a notation of "shirking," which means being lazy. This doesn't describe Dennis, as Dennis saw it, since he said he had a strong work ethic. He was only nineteen years old at that time and maybe he just didn't understand how life works yet, you can't get anywhere in life without having ambition, and I don't see this in Dennis at that time. He was more along the lines of if *I don't like something I'm not going to do it*, even though it may be necessary to get where he needed or wanted to be.

His second suicide attempt was while he was AWOL. He went to his friend's house and lay on the picnic table in his backyard, putting a gun to his head wanting to pull the trigger. He couldn't do it. We all know it's a cry for help, but what kind of help was he looking for? His other suicide attempts were fruitless.

While Dennis was working at the Short Stop, the Polries (the owners) had gotten to know him and had him doing some cleaning around the restaurant and then eventually had him help out being a fry cook. They trusted him enough to leave him in charge of the restaurant on a weekend. He was so close to them that they offered to give him $500 to buy some painting equipment. Dennis had odd jobs doing painting.

Dennis wasn't exactly an upstanding citizen. In June 1966, he attempted to rob a store in Richmond, California. When the cashier opened her drawer, he decided to take the money and bolt out the front door. He didn't get very far. The security guard had grabbed him in the parking lot. He was arrested for robbery and grand theft. It states the matter was dismissed and reduced to petty theft. He was sentenced to one-year probation with six months custody sentence suspended. He basically got a slap on the hand. He did no jail time. Had they known the other crimes he was to commit, maybe they would have sent him to jail. Maybe Susan and Caree would be alive today had he spent time in jail.

One thing that I can't understand is that Dennis's childhood was not fraught with abuse or neglect. He may not have gotten along with his father, but there was no sign or indication of any sort of abuse. I am sure his father was strict due to him being in the military. It makes me wonder if Dennis was just weak due to being a mama's boy. My son is somewhat of a mama's boy, but he can stand on his own two feet and survive without me because I have taught him that. You become independent, not codependent.

Dennis was different; I feel he thought he was owed somehow. Was he given what he wanted after each suicide attempt? Did he get everything he wanted when he acted out? Dennis was the older brother. Maybe his parents were not always around and left Dennis in charge of taking care of his brothers, and that is why he wanted so much attention. It's been known to happen in other cases. Unfortunately no one knows in this case.

Chapter Thirteen

On August 1, 1966, the day he killed the girls, Dennis had returned home from a trip to Los Angeles where he was looking for a job. When he got home, he saw that his wife had a party and that there was another man. He wasn't sure what to do, so he decided he wanted to go for a drive to get a cup of coffee, and that was when he came upon Susan and Caree.

He passed by them and then something came over him. He states that a rage came over him.

As he was backing up, he was telling himself, "You don't want to do this," but he didn't have control over his life at that point; he felt he had to do it. We know what became of these thoughts.

After he killed the girls, he returned to his house and told his wife, "I guess we can't work things out." Dennis had been working with his neighbor, George Willis, off and on in the past as a painter at the Alameda Naval Station. Dennis had gone over to George's house, but he wasn't home. Dennis told George's wife, Linda, to give his painting supplies to George and stated, "I'm quitting my job."

He then drove back to his house and preceded to give his wife some things he had, which included the .22 caliber pistol he had used on the girls. He had stolen the gun two to three weeks before this. She didn't even know he had a gun. Pamela wasn't comfortable with the gun, so she gave it to the Willis. Surprisingly, on August 6, George turned the gun over to the authorities after he found out what Dennis had done. I say surprisingly because Dennis and George were pretty close and some people take friendship as precedence over doing what is right.

Such was the case of Davon Crawford in March 2009 in Cleveland, Ohio. Davon was at home with his family. He was married with three kids, and his sister-in-law was also there. Davon just lost it and shot all of them. The youngest boy was on the front porch after being shot. Davon's best friend had heard about the shooting and went over to the house. He saw the child on the front porch injured and turned around and walked away because Davon was his best friend. It's too bad they didn't have a law where this could be considered some sort of crime. As a human being, how in the world could you turn your back on a child who is suffering because you feel loyal to your friend? This just infuriates me.

Dennis had also gone to see Mrs. Polries when he came back from Los Angeles. about three weeks earlier after looking for a job and had asked for a loan of $2,000, stating he wanted to consolidate his debts. She said they weren't able to help him because they didn't have that kind of money to loan.

After his crimes came to light, she stated, "Never once did I get the impression that Dennis was sick or wild." She had also left her daughters with him without hesitation. It makes you wonder how she felt when she knew all of the specifics of what Dennis had done.

Dennis left his house and drove around some more, going over in his mind what he did. He felt no remorse after taking the lives of two innocent teenage girls who were just on the edge of the best times of their lives. Dennis knew he couldn't go home at that point, so he proceeded to drive to San Francisco to look for a new job. He had slept in his truck during this time waiting to hear about a job he had applied for while there, but he heard nothing so he decided to drive back to Richmond instead of staying in his truck another night.

On Wednesday, August 3, 1966, things were going to change dramatically. While driving toward Richmond, he heard an announcement come on the radio that the police in Pinole had found the bodies of two girls that had been shot. That is when Dennis thought to himself, *Well, I'm going to go to jail so, I might as well take all I could.*

Chapter Fourteen

Around 8:30 that evening, he came upon eighteen-year-old Sherry Goldman (pseudonym) sitting in her car in the parking lot of a drug store at the Linda Mar shopping center in Pacifica. Right then Dennis decided he was going to kidnap and rape her. In Dennis's true fashion, he opened the door of her car on the passenger side and got in. He told her to drive him to his car that was broken down, the same story he gave his first victim, Jane Wallington. After she drove to his car, he took the keys out of the ignition, pulled out a knife, and demanded her money. She gave him her purse and there was only about $6.00 in it.

When they came to a stop he dragged her out of the driver's side of the car and bound her wrists along with her feet. This was a new one for Dennis; he had not bound the feet with the other victims. He used the same type of wire that he used on the other women and Emily.

He drove about five miles to a secluded beach near Devil's Slide and forced her down the hill. It was dark at this point so he knew he had plenty of privacy. He pushed her down to the beach via knifepoint.

He begins to order her to "Kiss me or I'm going to hurt you."

She said the same thing that every other woman has asked: "Why are you doing this?" She refused to kiss him.

"It doesn't matter why I'm doing this. Just do as I say," he commanded.

At this point, he removed the wire from her feet and started pulling at her blouse. It was at this point that she tried to escape and just started running. He ran after her and took the wire he had used to bind her feet and put it around her neck.

He threatened, "I'm going to kill you unless you stay quiet and do as I say."

She quieted down and at that point he tried to strangle her. She really had no other choice but to quiet down. She had nowhere to go. He started to rape her and when he was done he told her, "Wait here for five minutes after I leave." He then proceeded to steal her car and just left her there on the beach alone.

Her hands were loosely bound and she was able to get free. She put her clothes back on and ran up the hill to the highway to get some help and report it to the police. She was then taken to General Hospital for an examination. It was noted she had contusions, abrasions, and welts around her wrists where he had tied her with the wire.

As Dennis was driving back toward Pinole, a radio broadcast went out about 9:35 P.M. to keep an eye out for Sherry's car and her "assailant." The California Highway State Patrol had set up roadblocks around the city and around 11:30 P.M. they spotted the car with Dennis behind the wheel. Dennis was taken into custody without resistance.

When they located his own truck, they found a sleeping bag, a wood-handled pocketknife, a thirteen-inch bolo knife, and two other pocketknives. His knife of choice looked like a linoleum knife. The blade of this knife was curved, not straight like a regular knife. This was the same knife used on all the other victims. The Pacifica Police Chief, Neil Tremaine, stated the eighteen-year-old victim was able to identify Dennis as her rapist and he was subsequently jailed in San Mateo County.

I would imagine at this point Dennis was somewhat relieved for all of it to be over with; he really had nowhere to go. He had a falling out with his wife, he gave all of his stuff to George, and he knew he would have to pay for the crimes against Susan and Caree because the police would end up figuring it out.

After spending a night in jail in San Mateo, he was arraigned in North County Municipal Court on felony charges of kidnapping, armed robbery, and auto theft for the crimes against eighteen-year-old Sherry. The kidnaping charge was a capital offense, which is punishable by death. So, just on that charge alone Dennis was looking at death. When Dennis appeared before Judge F. Jose de

Larios, he did not have an attorney, so the judge moved the hearing until the next day, August 5, so the court could appoint an attorney for Dennis. At the time, Dennis's bail was set at $10,000, which would be somewhere around $84,000 today. There was no way he could pay that. Court-appointed Attorney Robert Miller was ordered to represent Dennis.

One of the deputies from San Mateo County, Sergeant Paul Hart, after hearing of Dennis's crime, suggested the Contra Costa Sheriff's Deputies go question Dennis about the murder of Susan and attempted murder of Caree. At this time, Caree was still alive so he could only be charged with attempted murder. They didn't have any definitive evidence tying him to the crimes but the proximity of his home to Point Wilson and Susan's babysitting job in Pinole made them question him. After all, he was the neighbor to the Eddy's. They interrogated him but nothing became of it. Dennis admitted to nothing.

After they paid him a visit, Dennis had called a police officer friend of his to ask him for his advice on what to do. Dennis stated, "I was scared. You know, I wanted to talk to him and ask him for advice and what to do and all this. He was of no help..." Dennis does not name who this police officer was, but I am guessing the officer wanted no part of this and brushed him off. Or maybe legally he couldn't say anything since it was an ongoing investigation and he was a police officer.

Dennis was also identified by Jane Wallington as her attacker, so a hold was put on him for this crime. Contra Costa County put a hold on him for Susan and Caree as well. He fit the description given by the other victims as well as the knife he had used. He was called the "Linoleum Knife Rapist" by law enforcement because of it. Berkeley Albany Municipal Court issued a warrant for his arrest charging him with rape and kidnapping in Jane's case. This carried a bail of $22,000. Pacifica police said at least seven law enforcement agencies had made inquiries into Dennis.

Interestingly enough in this case, a twenty-one-year-old male had confessed to the murders of Susan and Caree so they had not looked at Dennis as the primary suspect in the beginning stages of the investigation. This youth wasted the time and resources of the officers who were trying to find the killer because it was a false confession and he had nothing to do with it. You hear of this often. There is always someone who will come forward with a confession knowing it was false, but they did so because they wanted attention. They don't understand how detrimental that can be for a case. It takes time away from finding the real killer and can also help the defense at trial. The defense can put reasonable doubt into a juror's mind by stating this other person had confessed to it, so it wasn't their client. I have heard of these instances many times.

Chapter Fifteen

On August 12, Contra Costa County sheriff filed a murder complaint against Dennis after speaking with him in jail in Redwood City and served it to him in jail. Sometime around 3:00 A.M., Dennis decided he wanted to talk to the authorities involved: Deputy District Attorney John Hatzenbuhler, from Contra Costa County; his own lawyer, Robert Miller; and Sheriff Richard Davis. They met for roughly an hour and a half. According to Dennis, he stated, "I don't feel I was responsible for what really happened. But I'll tell you all I know." He also at this time confessed to "four or five other rapes in Contra Costa County…I want to get them over with everything…I want no more of this." So, is this a sign of remorse or just defeat because he knew he was caught? I don't believe at this time Dennis felt any sort of remorse. When asked why he decided to shoot the girls, he stated, "I didn't decide. They were just all of a sudden dead." In later transcripts he will say differently. He ended his confession with, "I would like to see a doctor…I don't believe I was responsible for what I did." I'm not so sure I could keep my cool as an officer and not say "Are you kidding me? How can you think you weren't responsible? You were there and committed the crime." He described the girls as "beatniks with long hair," which was a word used to describe hippy types. Further into his confession, he makes the statement that he hopes the girls get medical attention. Is that remorse or just hope that he doesn't get charged with two murders? It can make you feel a little conflicted because you want to believe he has remorse, but how can you if it was so easy for you to commit the crimes to begin with?

At the conclusion of the confession, Dennis's attorney, Robert Miller, requested a physical and psychiatric examination, as well as an X-ray of his skull. Dennis's mom had told Mr. Miller that, "Dennis sustained a severe concussion as a boy and that he had not had further physical examination since that time." I would assume this is the incident when Dennis fell out of the car at three years old. It could be plausible that Dennis had sustained a head injury that changed his way of thinking of right or wrong, and impulse control. This type of excuse, as I would say, was not touched on again throughout Dennis's trial. I would assume it was never proven.

After his confession, alone in his cell, feeling overwhelmed and supposed remorse, Dennis tried to commit suicide. He had shoved a piece of coat hanger into a vein in his left arm. He was taken to the San Mateo County General Hospital where he received five stitches and was released back to his cell. According to the jail, he could not have gotten a coat hanger in the jail so they started looking at others who may have helped him get it. Honestly, with the crimes he was charged with, I wouldn't be surprised if someone wanted to help him commit suicide. We know this was not the first time he had tried to commit suicide and certainly won't be his last. So, it begs to question whether or not he actually meant to do it. He never seemed to accomplish any of his suicide attempts up to this point. When he returned to his cell, for some reason, he asked for a priest. It was said that a priest from Mt. Carmel parish in Redwood City had spent twenty minutes with him in private. Why now? Considering he was Mormon, it's not clear why he would ask for a priest. Why wouldn't he ask for one before he committed these crimes when he knew he wasn't doing well and felt the impulses of raping and killing women? Maybe if he had, he may not have committed these crimes. But, then again, was Dennis just destined to be evil?

Dennis was also questioned in another crime, the murder of Judy Williamson, which he denied any knowledge of. Judy's remains were discovered in a remote area of San Mateo, California, in April of 1966. Judy was a student at University of California at Berkeley who went missing while she was walking to classes from her home in Albany in 1963. She had been missing for three years by the time they found her remains. When Dennis was questioned by the Albany Police

Chief Ralph Jensen, he stated that Dennis appeared to be truthful, and Jensen dismissed it. It wasn't until 1978 that her murder was solved, after the son of the Albany Mayor confessed to the murder.

Chapter Sixteen

On August 15, District Attorney for Contra Costa County, John Nejedly, sent out notice to jurors to appear for a grand jury hearing on the following day at 7:30 P.M. The grand jury hearing lasted two days, and a twelve-count indictment was returned after hearing from nine witnesses: Dr. William Bogart, who was the pathologist for Susan's autopsy; Deputy Sheriff Douglas Young, who was the initial responding officer to the crime scene where they found the girls; Contra Costa criminalist John Thorton, who presented physical evidence; Dr. R Eugene Kreps, who was Caree's physician; the three girls he had previously assaulted; Sheriff's Sergeant Richard Davis; and John Sheldon, who was the witness from the convenience store that saw the girls get in the panel van. The jury was dismissed after testimony and only deliberated for ten minutes. He was charged with first degree murder for Susan Box (which carries the death penalty); kidnapping for robbery with injury, which is also an automatic death penalty; attempted murder for Caree, who was still alive at this point; four counts of kidnapping; three counts of forcible rape; one count of sexual perversion; and one count of robbery. The transcript of this hearing was sixty-six pages, but I have been unable to obtain a copy since it has been destroyed. According to news sources, speaking about the crime, Dennis stated, "One minute I'm sorry. The next I ain't."

On August 18, 1966, Dennis's wife, Pamela, had filed for a divorce on the grounds of extreme cruelty and causing her "embarrassment and distress." She asked for all of the marital property and custody of the four kids, although only two of them belonged to her and Dennis.

On the morning of August 19, 1966, Dennis appeared before Superior Court Judge Robert Cooney. His arraignment hearing had to be continued due to Dennis having no counsel, as well as the fact that by the law the Defendant is to have a copy of the transcript from the Grand Jury hearing and the transcript would not be ready for at least another few days. Judge Cooney appointed Vance Porlier to defend him.

He appeared for his arraignment hearing on August 24, 1966, where he was given a copy of the transcript. His attorney respectfully asked to have his hearing scheduled for a week later, on August 31, 1966, to enter his pleas to the twelve-count indictment.

He appeared again before Judge Robert Cooney of the Contra Costa Superior Court on August 31 to enter his plea of guilty or not guilty. His attorney, Robert Miller, entered a plea of not guilty by reason of insanity on Dennis's behalf and requested a psychological evaluation, which the judge granted. If you are any sort of superstitious or don't believe in coincidences, it is interesting that during this hearing the lights in the courtroom had suddenly gone out for about five minutes and came back on, with no explanation. Was this a sign of some sort? What if the five minutes was how long Susan lived after she was shot? Maybe I'm reaching a bit, but imagine if that were true.

Judge Cooney then ordered Dennis to undergo a psychological evaluation at Napa State Hospital to determine his mental competence to stand trial. The examination was going to take around three weeks. Two psychiatrists were ordered to examine him, Dr. Reginald Rood and Dr. Amino Perretti, and they were to report their findings to the court at the hearing on September 22. At this time Vance Porlier was appointed as Dennis's attorney for the trial. If he was determined to be insane, he would be confined to a state institution instead of prison. Honestly, being in an institution would be a god-send compared to prison because they keep you so medicated, you don't even know what is going on and therefore you can escape reality.

According to Dr. Reginald Rood's report, "Stanworth's problem was not in the area of knowledge and understanding, but in the area of self-control in the face of abnormal sexual predispositions from non-psychotic personality disorders." Dr. Amino Perritti stated in his report that Dennis "admitted to molesting his seven-year-old daughter and to being a peeping tom." It would come out later that his wife, Pamela, did not believe him when it came to him admitting molestation. He's admitting to this and she says she doesn't believe him? She testified, "I don't believe that ever happened." She said her daughter was normal and loved her father. I was also "normal" after it happened to me. Signs of a child being molested are much more prevalent now because it is something parents talk to their children about, and parents warn their children what can happen to them by sexual predators. When we were kids that wasn't something that was talked about. It was taboo, "that doesn't happen." There are millions of kids who would certainly disagree with that.

I have reached out to Pamela's family to see if there is a misunderstanding about this or she definitely didn't believe him, but I couldn't get anyone with direct knowledge of this, including Pamela, to speak to me. So, I have to go by what's included in the record. If true, there is something seriously wrong with this woman. If he had committed the rapes of two teenagers, then why not a seven year old? Dennis, of course, denies this later.

Chapter Seventeen

On September 20, 1966, Dennis, again, went before the Grand Jury of Contra Costa County for a second indictment for first-degree murder for the murder of Caree Collison, who had passed away September 12. He was, again, ordered to stand trial for her murder as well. Also at this indictment, an attorney, Vance Porlier, was assigned and $350.00 was ordered to provide Dennis an opportunity to seek a psychiatrist of his own choosing. So, the State of California gives you money to get your psychological examination. That would explain why California is a financial mess.

On Friday, September 23, 1966, Dennis went to court again to decide his mental competency. Judge Cooney, after reading the medical exam reports, ruled that Dennis "is presently sane and understands the nature of the proceedings," and a jury trial was set for December 5, 1966. This was a huge win for the prosecution and the people of California. Dennis would not be going to some hospital for years getting treatment, but instead was going to be behind bars, where he was no longer in control of anything but his bowels. And, at some point in the future, he would no longer be in charge of those either.

On September 29, 1966, Dennis entered his pleas to the first indictment of not guilty by reason of insanity, but on the counts of kidnapping, aggravated kidnapping, and robbery he pled not guilty, but not with the reason of insanity. The first indictment included the murder of Susan and attempted murder of Caree, but since Caree ultimately died, the attempted murder charge had been upgraded to murder, for which brought about the second indictment. He pled not guilty by reason of insanity to the second indictment for her murder. The Court ultimately combined both indictments into one case, rather than try them separately.

After some time sitting in jail thinking about what he had done, Dennis again tried to commit suicide on October 5. He had taken a razor blade and slashed his arm. Authorities stated there was a suicide note but would not divulge what was in it. He was taken to the local hospital and returned to his cell.

Adding a twist to this case, on November 14, 1966, Dennis changed his pleas. He pled guilty to all charges. He pled guilty to all counts that were listed in the indictments: two counts of murder, one count of kidnapping to commit robbery with bodily harm, four counts of kidnapping, three counts of forcible rape, one count of sexual perversion, and one count of robbery. Both murders were of first degree, which carried a death sentence. I guess at this point Dennis decided the court was not going to work in his favor and gave up. Or did he feel so much remorse he wanted to get it over with?

Dennis wanted to waive his right to a jury trial and go straight to the penalty phase. According to court documents, Dennis's attorney, Vance Porlier, stated to the Court that Dennis was not being cooperative and just wanted to "get it over with." Dennis also asked that the penalty phase be decided by the judge. Judge Gregg stated, "In the best interests of justice the court should not try this case..." He denied the request and jury selection proceeded to take place on November 30, 1966.

Eighty-one members were called for jury duty, which consisted of forty-five women and thirty-six men. Twenty-two of these were dismissed from having to decide Dennis's fate. Twelve members stated they were opposed to the death penalty and ten others had already made up their minds to the penalty they would give. This will play a very important factor in Dennis's case when it came to his appeals. Some jurors made the statement that it would be an "awesome task" to decide Dennis's fate. Carl Kurvers was one juror that had to excuse himself because Dennis had spent a considerable amount of time at the motorcycle dealership where Mr. Kurvers's daughter worked. His daughter stated to him that Dennis was well liked and "mild mannered."

Nonetheless, the final jury panel chosen consisted of six men and six women, with two alternates. It was said that Dennis just sat there unphased by the proceedings and even doodled on a crushed paper cup. I wonder what was going through his mind. Maybe he had a sense of denial, or maybe he just didn't care about the decision the jury was going to make because he was ready to die.

On November 19, 1966, around 1:40 A.M., Dennis again tried to commit suicide by the same method he had tried previously. Dennis had broken off half of a razor blade while shaving and then put the rest of the blade back into the razor in order to make it look normal. Dennis had placed a sheet on his cell floor to lie on as he slashed his left arm below the elbow. He was discovered by a cellmate when he heard Dennis moaning and saw him on the floor. He had lost a considerable amount of blood, but they were able to get him to the hospital before he bled out. Corporal Robert Fisher of the sheriff's department stated Dennis had been saving this razor "for a rainy day." He had been given a blood transfusion at the hospital since he had lost so much blood and was sent back to the jail. No matter what he tried, he was never successful in his suicide attempts. It makes you wonder if God was behind that. Did he actually spare him for some sort of purpose? What would that purpose be? No one will ever know.

Chapter Eighteen

During the penalty phase trial, the prosecution would call witnesses to testify as to Dennis's character and to explain or make the jury understand how the death penalty was appropriate for the crimes he committed. Four of his victims (Jane Wallington, Emily Duncan, Pamela Scott, and Sherry Goldman) testified to what Dennis had done to them. They were the only ones to speak on Caree and Susan's behalf. The courage it must have taken to face him in the courtroom and point their finger at him in order to identify the "Linoleum Knife Rapist.. Some of them may have also been thankful they were spared by Dennis, but unfortunately Susan and Caree were not.

The Box and Collison families attended the hearing. According to the Collison family, Caree's Uncle Verne wanted to jump the rail that divided the public seating from the attorneys and criminals and go after Dennis. Caree was like a daughter to him; of course there would be an enormous amount of anger. One thing that must have been very hard for the Box family was to look at the pictures presented by the prosecution of Susan with the wounds she sustained. The pictures showed her bullet wounds and other scratches she sustained. Of course, Dennis's attorney objected due to the gruesomeness and said it could "inflame the jury." Judge Norman Gregg overruled his objection and allowed the pictures. It was stated that Susan had traces of tranquilizers in her system, although I could not find this notated in the coroner's report I received.

The defense called their own witnesses: Dennis's mother, Nellie; his wife, Pamela; close friend, George Willis; Dennis's mother-in-law, Mary Button; and surprisingly, Dennis himself. George Willis had turned over the gun to police that Pamela had given to George's wife, which was the murder weapon, so it is very interesting that the defense would call him as a witness. I would think most close friends would cover for the other, but George Willis did the right thing.

Dennis's mother took the stand in his defense and relayed to the court that Dennis was a good kid until he went into the Army. She said something had significantly changed with him. But my question is how? He was only in the Army for six months and did not see combat. Being former military myself, it doesn't add up. Basic training is a mind game and physically challenging, but in no way is it detrimental, especially in today's world where kids are coddled. But she also stated he needed to be "babied all the time." So, he was one that needed attention, and what better way to get attention than to rape and kill women? In my opinion he was just plain weak. I do not coddle grown men; they just need to suck it up and go on.

His mother testified that "No mother could ask for a better boy." She also went on to say that he was one of the most ambitious boys she had known, and a good son. At one point she tried to justify or explain the reason he was the way he ended up being by explaining that Dennis had sustained a concussion as a child, which went untreated. This could possibly be true. He had fallen out of the car when he was three years old and had to be treated at the hospital. So, it begs the question of whether or not Dennis was the way he was because he had damaged the part of the brain that controls your judgment and impulses, or was he just naturally mentally damaged?

During witness testimony, Dennis just looked down at the table with his hands clenched, but glanced at his mother a couple of times. How would a mother feel being on the stand defending her son's character knowing what he had done to innocent women? Maybe in those days she felt it was the right thing to do. I hope it wasn't out of guilt, because nothing points to her or his father on why he did what he did. Did she try to tell herself that it was her fault and now she wanted to correct it? Too many times you hear of people blaming their childhood as to why they turned out the way they did. I don't play that card or buy that. A *lot* of people go through bad childhoods and don't end up as killers, so why try to feel sorry for this one? In my opinion, it's all about choices. You choose to do good or evil, and Dennis chose evil, no matter how you want to spin it. What he did had nothing to do with his mother or father.

His friend, George, told the jury, "I still like the guy as much as I did before." I would think there should be some sort of disdain toward Dennis for what he had done. How can you not? He killed two fifteen-year-old girls and raped one of them, *after* she was deceased, not to mention the four other women he assaulted.

Dennis's wife, Pamela, stated that she "couldn't have asked for a better husband." Pamela said they were writing back and forth while he was in jail and he told her they needed to get a divorce so she could go on with her life. According to Dennis, Pamela knew of Dennis's thirst for rape. The year before Dennis had attempted to kidnap and rape a woman, but when the woman screamed Dennis ran off. Dennis actually told Pamela of this incident and her comment was that if he were to feel some sort of sexual need they just need to get together and have sex to take care of that need. It is very hard for me to not be angry with her. Dennis also stated later on that he would not approach her sexually unless she was bound. At some point you would really wonder what was off with Dennis; obviously there were signs she chose to ignore. Had she reported these incidents, these other women and the girls would not have suffered the pain they did at the hands of her husband. I was unable to get any sort of rebuttal from Pamela on this.

According to onlookers, Dennis was choked up and quivering when the prosecution played the confession tape to the jury. During his wife's testimony, they stated it looked like he was crying. He stated he confessed to the murders because, "I couldn't live with it anymore. I told everything I did." He went on to say, "I always was sorry after I got through," which goes to what he had said to Jane Wallington after he raped her. When asked by his attorney if it was true that he was sometimes sorry and other times not, Dennis broke down, sobbing, saying, "I don't know anymore. I've been thinking for five months and I just don't know." Dennis asked Judge Gregg if he could make a statement. I would have to give the judge kudos for declining his request. What more could Dennis possibly say? *Sorry* would not take away the pain the victims and families felt.

One of the psychiatrists who evaluated him as to his sanity stated Dennis had a history of "abnormal sexual attitudes" since Dennis was a young teenager.

He stated this included molesting young girls, indecent exposure, and voyeurism (basically a peeping tom), and that he showed a sadistic attitude toward women. Did anyone happen to notice anything strange or off about Dennis? It doesn't seem like it. From the sounds of it, he seemed completely normal, except that his wife had to know something was off. There's no way she could have thought it was normal to only have sex if you're bound by your own husband.

After four days of testimony from both the prosecution and defense, the jury was dismissed to deliberate. It only took them four and a half hours to decide that the appropriate sentence for Dennis was the death penalty. Judge Gregg read the sentences aloud. "In count one, a first-degree murder charge, the sentence is death by the administration of a lethal gas within the walls of the state prison at San Quentin." He was also given life without the chance of parole for the crime against Emily Duncan. After the ruling, the judge stated, "I suppose there is nothing I can really say; however, on two occasions during the trial you wanted to say something. Is there anything you wish to say now?" To which Dennis answered, "No, sir."

Dennis's wife, Pamela, sat behind Dennis in the courtroom with a priest as support. Even though she had asked for a divorce and was basically moving on, she still came to his sentencing hearing as a supportive wife. She touched his hand before they took him away. I can't begin to put myself in her shoes, but in the face of all of the evidence in this case and his confessions, I am not so sure I would have stood by him, and if I did I certainly wouldn't do it publicly. I don't know if she stayed living in Pinole, but I would have moved, well before he even went to trial. I am sure the media was all over her and putting her under a microscope as well. She knew it had to be true, he admitted to it, and the evidence was too much for her to deny his guilt.

After the hearing, Dennis shook his attorney's hand and was led back to jail. In the State of California, if you are sentenced to death, it is an automatic appeal, whether the Defendant wants to appeal the sentence or not. Dennis requested the death penalty. He wanted to die because he was "bringing shame on my family name." I would imagine there would have been a lot of shame toward him from his father, who was a war hero.

Dennis was then moved to death row at San Quentin, overlooking San Francisco Bay. I drove this route to see what Dennis had seen that day. I am sure there are quite a few differences between then and now as far as how desolate it is, but I wanted to experience a part of it.

The drive was nothing I expected; it was actually quite beautiful. After passing over the Golden Gate Bridge, you come into a mountainous region that was just full of greenery. That may not have been the case for Dennis since he was transferred on December 7 during the winter and I had visited in February. You see the sign for San Quentin and take a left onto the road leading there. There are no other roads there, just one straight, narrow road to the prison. Currently there are numerous places of residence. I was quite shocked considering the prison is right there and you never know what could happen. The best I could explain is the housing belongs to those who work for the prison. The view I had in mind before arriving was one of a big parking lot and the prison off in the distance surrounded with fencing and barbed wire, like all of the ones you have driven by or seen on TV. This is not what I encountered.

The road you are driving on is very narrow with cars parked on the side of the street. One side of the street is housing, and the other side goes off the cliff. The front gate of San Quentin is simply a wooden gate. I couldn't drive too close because the guard was very suspicious, and I didn't want to cause any issues. I got a small glimpse to the other side when the gate was opened. Inside the gate you see more homes, but the best I could tell none of the prison itself was visible. Outside the gate on the left was a little office that also held a soda machine as well as a visitor parking lot. In my mind, I'm thinking, *I can't imagine what it would be like during visitation hours.*

When you look across the bay at San Quentin, it is actually a very beautiful prison. It has sort of an Aztec look to it. Imagine being a prisoner knowing you will never be able to experience the beauty of the Bay or the many things to do in San Francisco because you are stuck behind those cold walls. I could imagine seeing across the Bay after the fog lifted and the sun appeared. I am sure it is breathtaking, but even worse for a prisoner. I think this view in itself is torture. Their choices put them there so that is their punishment.

Just to give you an idea of others who were already on death row, there were Clyde Bates and Manuel Chavez. On April 4, 1957, these two men lit a bar on fire, killing six people and injuring one. They were found guilty on six counts of murder and one count of arson. In 1971, Charles Manson arrived at San Quentin and was also on death row. It makes you wonder if they ever spoke to each other. In his own right Charles was famous, but Dennis was never on anyone's radar as far as what he had done, and was even more heinous than what Charles Manson did, in my opinion. I am not downplaying the murders he had his followers do, but I believe the difference in the severity of it is that two young teenage girls were killed. They were never to experience graduating high school or even going to the prom. They may never have kissed a boy yet, and the innocence of being a teenager was essentially stolen from them.

Chapter Nineteen

In March 1967, Dennis's appeal was filed by his attorney, J. Vance Porlier, with the California Supreme Court stating the prosecutor and judge had made irreversible errors during Dennis's first trial and asked that his death sentence be overturned. One of the arguments had to deal with the pictures that were shown of the body of Susan Box and how "gruesome" they were. He also alleged that the judge did not instruct the jury to disregard any statements regarding Dennis's past offenses. The whole thing about this that can make you somewhat angry is the fact that Dennis didn't want to appeal his case at all, or have his case overturned. This was the attorney's choice to save Dennis's butt from execution. I am having a hard time not being angry with his defense attorneys. If your client is flat-out guilty and has confessed, then why bother trying to save their life? What sort of good can come of that? In this case, I wonder if he would regret arguing to save Dennis's life if he knew what things were to come.

In a strange move on Dennis's part, he had written a letter to the Supreme Court of California asking them to dismiss his appeal. He had asked the court to dismiss his attorney so Dennis could dismiss his own appeal since his attorney would not and could not. This request was denied. The Court stated, "such efforts on defendant's part were not based on any dissatisfaction with any action or conduct of such counsel or with his abilities or skills as an attorney, but instead were predicated upon the defendant's desire not to be represented at all."

During this time, Dennis must have done his homework on the legal system and how things were supposed to be done and how to file correctly. On June 15, 1967, he filed with the Court a Voluntary Abandonment of Appeal. This is a request to dismiss his appeal, but Dennis did this on his own, without the knowledge of his attorney. Since it was written with the correct legal language and within the California rule of law, the Court had to consider the motion. The Court asked Dennis's attorney and prosecution to submit briefs regarding the Motion. Dennis had also written to the Attorney General with an Affidavit of Verification, which is basically his written confession, and had it notarized. He gave this to them to include in their brief to the Supreme Court to push the issue that Dennis didn't want an appeal and wanted to just have the death penalty and be done with all of it. In this Dennis writes, "I DENNIS STANWORTH hereby swear that the conviction which has resulted in the sentence of death is valid. I also swear that no violation of my constitutional rights has taken place; and if any have, I waive those rights. I stipulate that the record of my trial is valid and the contentions of the respondent are true and that the contentions as put to this court in my briefs have no merit."

The Supreme Court acknowledged the fact that Dennis's intentions were to dismiss his attorney and the appeal in order that "he may suffer." The Court had denied his request for dismissal of his attorney and appeal. Dennis could not understand why they wouldn't dismiss his attorney or dismiss his appeal. His statement to the court was he pled guilty; he was even giving them his life, so why does he have to go through this? He also seemed to be concerned about all of this being in the newspapers. He seemed more concerned about his reputation and the reputation of his family. He stated, "I know that I will never see the freedom of the outside world again. I have dishonored my family's name, not to mention the pain and agony to myself and my wife…I wish to cause no more expense to the state with the legal fees and cost of housing."

So, as admirable as it is that he wanted to protect his family and accept death, you still have to remember the crimes he committed and how the girls suffered, all of them. Why should he be exempt from suffering? In my opinion, death is not punishment. From my Christian beliefs, death is a reprieve from the evil in this world. I am not afraid to die, just afraid of leaving my child without a mother. Dennis needs to suffer, not be given a reprieve from emotional pain by giving him death. On the other hand, you also feel like what a waste of a person, and why should we keep him alive and continue to spend money on him? It is not cheap to keep someone alive in prison for years and years. Prisons in today's world offer inmates a lot of free opportunities, such as getting degrees and free medical care. But we work hard day in and day out and have to pay for it out of pocket, which most times a lot of us can't afford. That is one of the things I don't agree with. Even if they have these degrees, it is hard for them to even get a job to use that degree. Once you have the mark of being in prison, the chances of you getting hired is very slim, especially for violent crimes.

In a surprising move on August 20, 1969, the Supreme Court of CA ordered a new penalty phase trial for Dennis, along with five other men. In 1968 the case of Witherspoon v. Illinois (1968) 291 [71 Cal2d 826] U.S. 510 [20 L.E.2d 776, 88 S. Ct. 1770] was the reason they got new trials. It stated that you couldn't dismiss jurors based on whether they believe in the death penalty. Rather, they should be asked if they could render a death sentence based on all of the evidence, and not just from their personal feelings. For example, one of the jurors, Mr. Muldoon, was asked on his questionnaire whether he believed in the death penalty and he indicated he did not, therefore, he was excused from being a juror to decide whether or not Dennis would get the death penalty. I can understand this from the prosecutor's perspective. The prosecution wanted the death penalty and certainly wasn't going to take a chance on whether or not a juror can decide on the penalty of death.

The death penalty is a very touchy subject in society. I don't really have a preference either way. The main issue I would have is I would need to be absolutely 100 percent sure that the person is guilty. There are far too many people in prison that are innocent. I wouldn't want the burden of deciding death unless the evidence was rock solid, such as cases with DNA. DNA doesn't lie, although I am sure there are cases where DNA is planted.

One of the other arguments was that the pictures presented at the first trial of the girls were too gruesome and had no value since the Defendant already confessed to what happened. During this trial, the defense had objected to the inclusion of the photos but the objection was overruled, and the photographs were included.

The pictures were all of Susan, and no pictures of Caree lying in a hospital bed. The photos of Susan were taken at the crime scene and at the morgue. They only showed her legs, back, buttocks, and her left arm, which was twisted up over her back. The ones taken in the morgue did not show the gunshot wound to her head, only the numerous other injuries she sustained. Dennis had denied any of the torture that was speculated by the law enforcement and medical community, which they believe the torture contributed to her numerous bruises and scratches. Some felt this might have been sustained when he dragged her to place her with Caree underneath the brush. It makes you wonder if Dennis hated seeing these pictures because he had some sort of remorse, or was it only a legal ploy that these pictures would be prejudicial to the jury? Dennis's attorney felt the pictures had no value in the case since Dennis pled guilty. Frankly I hope he did see them and had to live with those images the rest of his life.

The Court went on to state that as another fault in the penalty phase trial, "[w]e deal with the erroneous instruction that the prosecutor (Mr. Hatzenbuhler) with commendable candor has called to our attention. During a general instruction on the province and function of the jury the court stated, 'The law forbids you to be governed by sentiment, conjecture, sympathy, passion, prejudice, public opinion, or any other factor other than the evidence and the law.' It is an error to instruct the jury during a penalty phase of the trial that it cannot be governed or influenced by pity or sympathy for the defendant." In layman's terms, this means you can't decide whether or not someone is guilty by your emotions during the trial. It must be based upon the evidence in the case, *except* during the penalty phase.

In summary of the ruling, most of the judges rendered the same opinion: the judgments against Dennis would stand, but he was entitled to a new penalty phase trial. This was a win for both sides, in my opinion. He would still be charged with the same crimes, but another jury would need to determine whether he got the death penalty, life with chance of parole, or life without the chance of parole.

In retrospect, the Court had no idea what the ramifications of this decision would be. It makes you wonder sometimes if judges feel any sort of guilt when they overturn a case or sentence, and that person goes on to commit another crime. If a female judge has a daughter, does that affect the outcome of a decision? Would she want her daughter to die at the hands of this man? The judges are the ones who make the decisions. But does a female judge base their opinion more on feelings or the law? The men absolutely rule based upon the law. How can a female's emotions not enter into a judgment? It would certainly be hard to separate the two.

Chapter Twenty

The other three prisoners on death row that were also given new penalty trials due to the same reasons as Dennis's case were Harry Schader, Charles Gardner, and Booker Hillery.

Harold Schader shot Sacramento Police Officer Eugene McKnight on July 23, 1963. Charles Gardner beat to death Gerald Bispo, who owned a clothing store, on July 31, 1967. Booker Hillery stabbed to death Marlene Miller, who was fifteen years old, with a pair of scissors in 1965.

So, here are your most upstanding citizens (sarcastically said) being awarded new penalty trials, where they may have the opportunity for parole at some point in their life. Sure, I would like them as a neighbor. How does anyone feel about something like that? They would be very angry if this person ended up as their next-door neighbor.

Before the trial, Dennis would be transferred from San Quentin death row to the Contra Costa County jail. Initially Dennis's attorney, William Higham, requested that Dennis be transferred to the jail in Martinez, California, instead of back to San Quentin due to the travel time and getting Dennis prepared for trial. The judge who presided over the hearing, Superior Court Judge Richard Arnason, denied the request after he was told the jail in Martinez was overcrowded, so Dennis was returned to San Quentin.

Dennis wanted to act as his own attorney in the re-trial of his death sentence trial. Dennis's first attorney, Vance Porlier, had asked to be excused from being his attorney due to a two-year illness and stated, "My condition is such that I would not be capable" to handle the penalty phase trial. After this statement, Superior Court Judge Martin E. Rothenberg assigned public defender William Higham as Dennis's attorney. Mr. Higham advised the court that Dennis did not want him as his attorney unless he handled his case like Dennis wanted. Mr. Higham stated, "But it is not consistent with my duties as an attorney to my client to do this."

The judge had called them into chambers and asked Dennis if he did, in fact, not want to be represented. The judge read from the Supreme Court ruling that Dennis would not be allowed to act on his own behalf because he wanted to be executed. Dennis stated, "But I just don't understand how—the purpose of this (hearing), I mean I pleaded guilty. I confessed. I'll even give you my life. I'll sign my own death warrant. I just want to keep all of this garbage out of the papers." That's a very interesting statement. Does he want it out of the paper due to his own shame? At one point he had stated he didn't want to shame his family. So, was he looking out for himself or his family? I would imagine as a parent and family member you would most certainly want it out of the papers, but that was not to happen. The people in his life, I believe, were the ultimate sufferers. According to a family member, Dennis's father had gone into seclusion after Dennis's crimes. The shame of being the parent of a person who could do such a thing must have been great, but it was no fault of Stan or Nellie's. Dennis chose to do what he did.

Dennis filed a motion with the court to withdraw his guilty pleas for the deaths of Susan and Caree and a hearing was set for February 26, 1970. He filed these motions stating he had not given his pleas voluntarily. Judge Aranson denied this request and the second penalty phase trial was scheduled for June 15, 1970.

Chapter Twenty-One

For his second penalty phase trial, Attorney John Higham needed to prove to the jury that Dennis was mentally unbalanced at the time of the murders. He needed them to see that Dennis was "deranged" and "possessed." During this hearing, the prosecuting attorney, John Hatzenbuhler, called psychiatric witnesses who stated that even though Dennis was a "sexual psychopath," he was legally sane at the time of the murders. In a nutshell, a sexual psychopath is one who has sexual impulses they cannot control.

As the hearing began, Assistant Defense Attorney, Permilia Hulse, submitted a motion for immediate judgment for a sentence of life imprisonment, which was denied. She stated that to give him the death penalty four years after the crime would be "cruel and unusual punishment" because of psychological issues it could cause. As if Dennis didn't already have psychological issues. I don't think it would matter at that point.

The attorneys had learned their lesson on questioning potential jurors about the death penalty. They tread very lightly with their questions and with juror dismissals. It took about three days before they finally had a jury picked. The final jury consisted of six men and six women.

The same witnesses for the prosecution in Dennis's first trial were called again. This time a young lady, who was twenty-four at the time of the offense, testified that Dennis had tried to attack her but she screamed and he ran. This is the girl Dennis had told Pamela about for his first attempt to assault a woman.

Dennis's attorney stated in court that Dennis was a "man possessed" when he committed the murders and that normally Dennis was a good person. He was just mentally insane when he committed the acts. Mentally insane can mean a lot of things, both legally and clinically. Due to this being of legal nature, it basically stated that Dennis didn't know what he was doing at the time of the murders and couldn't differentiate between right or wrong due to a mental defect. That defense works very little in today's society, in my opinion. When a crime is so unjust and unexplainable, a defense attorney will claim mental insanity. How can we wrap our heads around such heinous acts? They have to be crazy to do something like that, right? Well, in my opinion, a lot of that is just smoke being blown you know where. After years of reading and watching true crime, I have come to believe that people can just be evil without being mentally insane. Everyone is capable of murder; it's whether you *choose* to do so. It is a choice and sometimes people choose wrong, mental defect or not. Of course, Dennis's attorney would call his own experts regarding Dennis's state of mind at the time in order to prove that he was insane.

One of the first witnesses the defense called to establish that he was not of right mind when he committed the crimes was a teacher and friend of Dennis's, Morris Benezra. Dennis was his art student as well as the newspaper boy, and he felt that Dennis was a part of his family when he was young. Also called was Dr. William D. Pierce, who stated that Dennis had "paranoid delusions" and his issues stemmed from childhood. Dennis felt women were out to get him. He suggested that Dennis's father "chided" him about his sex as a child. So, it makes me wonder if Dennis had questioned his sexual preference at a young age.

Surprisingly Dennis took the stand in his own defense. That is an extreme gamble. He told the jury that he didn't want to die anymore from murdering the girls but felt he deserved to. To me, that's just garnering sympathy from the jury. But his next statement would eviscerate any sympathy he may have had. As to Susan and Caree, he stated, "I saw them there and I thought 'you dirty lousy bitches. I'm going to kill you.' I hated them. I hated what they'd done to me." He was speaking of two teenage girls! They were innocent of everything. And yet, in his mind, he felt they were the enemy. Dennis's mother doted on him and even went to his trial to beg for his life, so please tell me how he came up with such hatred? Was it due to his questioning his own sexuality? He goes on to state that had he looked at them as human beings he would have felt sorry. But, because he saw them as females, he "cannot feel sorry."

Closing arguments were given on July 3, and instructions by the judge were given to the jury to deliberate Dennis's fate. The only two penalties that could be given was life imprisonment or death. During their deliberations, they had asked to hear the first taped confession from Dennis's original confession on August 3, 1966. On July 5, ten minutes after noon, the jury announced their punishment of Dennis: death, again. On July 29, the Court officially sentenced Dennis to death. There was no one in attendance on Dennis's behalf. He sat alone receiving his fate. Dennis immediately asked to be returned to San Quentin rather than the county jail. He had stated the jail was overcrowded.

Once again, since he received the death penalty, it was an automatic appeal to the CA Supreme Court.

So, Dennis was returned to San Quentin to live out his days looking out the window and seeing the beautiful San Francisco Bay—or does he?

Chapter Twenty-Two

Life went on for the rest of the Stanworth family, although his father never completely recovered from Dennis's crimes. How would a mother or father feel about their son being on death row for the killing of two teenage girls? I'm not even sure I would have wanted to use my last name. I am sure life was not easy having that last name after that. For some time, I am sure they were looked at as the killer's parents, with people not knowing how much the Stanworths were not at fault for what Dennis became.

They still traveled to Utah to Stan's parents, and he continued to provide for the family while working for Douglas Aircraft in Santa Monica.

Dennis was twenty-seven years old in 1970 after his second trial and returned to San Quentin's death row. He would spend the next two years of his life living on death row until a major ruling from the CA Supreme Court in 1972 would be in Dennis's favor, as well as 173 other death row inmates around the country.

In 1972, the CA State Supreme Court, as well as the U.S. Supreme Court, ruled that the death penalty was unconstitutional. This was based upon the case of *Furman v. Georgia* (408 U.S. 238 (1972). In a nutshell, the Supreme Court felt that the death penalty was in violation of the Eighth Amendment of the Constitution, which prohibits cruel and unusual punishments. It was also a violation of the Fourteenth Amendment, which is a citizen's rights to equal protection of the law. In this case, Furman, who was black, was in the middle of committing a home invasion when the owner interrupted him, and as Furman was running out the door the gun fell out of his hand, striking the owner and killing him. The Court felt that Furman's color and being poor was part of the reason he received the death penalty. The outcome put a stop to the death penalty in a majority of the states for four years. In California, the Supreme Court had decided the death penalty was also cruel and unusual punishment in the case of *People of the State of CA v. Anderson* (493 P.2d 880, 6 Cal. 3d 628 (Cal. 1972). This decision affected the death sentences of roughly 107 prisoners on death row at the time, including Dennis. After this ruling, on March 8, 1972, Dennis was moved to the general population at San Quentin, where he could live his life everyday among others, having hobbies (which he made money off of) and eventually have a job within the prison system. He would also receive therapy.

During Dennis's time at San Quentin, he obtained an associate's degree in data processing through Solano Community College. One of the professors was a close friend of a friend of Susan's sister, Carol. When he walked into class, he was shocked by what he saw. Dennis looked like any other man during those days; he did not look like a monster. It was a very eerie feeling, but he had a job to do, so he had to overlook it. I'm sure at times he just wanted to ask Dennis why? Why did he do those evil things to the girls, as well as the other women? Honestly, I don't even think Dennis knows why he did it, other than out of anger toward women. That is an explanation I don't completely understand about Dennis. From everything I have read and from the people I have spoken with, Dennis had never been wronged by the women in his life, other than the possible cheating of his wife. To be that angry and take it out on two fifteen-year-olds is inconceivable.

Dennis achieved quite a bit in prison. Not only did he earn an associate's degree in Liberal Arts, he also worked for the psychiatry department for a year. He also participated in the cable car program, where they would build miniature cable cars made out of walnut and sell them in the prison store. Dennis was also the shipping clerk at the prison warehouse, where he earned twenty-five cents an hour. That's not a lot, but certainly helpful while you are in prison.

Regarding Dennis's legal status, his case went before the Supreme Court of California, again, in 1974. This was due to the automatic appeals process to his second death penalty hearing, not because he requested it. Keep in mind that the death sentence was deemed unconstitutional in 1972, so that was also in play with this hearing. The Court rendered its opinion on June 3, 1974.

The first charge they considered was the kidnapping with robbery charge against Ms. Duncan. The People (Attorney General's office) disputed that the distance that Ms. Duncan was dragged by Dennis increased her risk of harm, which I completely agree with. He dragged her into a field, in the dark, where no one could see them in order to assault her. The Court stated, "(t)here is no evidence that the relatively brief movement of the victim here removed her from public view or in any other manner substantially increased the risk, beyond that inherent in the underlying crimes, that she could suffer physical harm," so the Court overturned his conviction. How much is that a slap in the face to Ms. Duncan? Basically, they are saying, *Sorry, he didn't drag you far enough to assault you so, therefore, he can't be convicted.* This is only the first of *many* injustices in this case.

The second argument pertained to the four kidnapping charges. The two kidnapping charges for Susan and Caree stood due to Dennis driving them to another location and forcing them up to the bluff by gunpoint. You can't really argue this wasn't kidnapping. On the other two charges they also let the charges stand, so at least he didn't get out of the kidnapping charges.

The next issue was the rape conviction. Dennis stated that the "rape" of a dead person cannot be considered rape, and this charge needed to be dismissed. But one problem was that Dennis had already pled guilty to that charge. You can't go back now and argue that it wasn't rape when you pled guilty to it. The coroner stated that death was almost "instantaneous." Dennis stated to his psychologist that while he was raping Susan, he heard her screaming, but retracted that statement at his second penalty trial stating it was he who was screaming. The Court just basically couldn't come to a decision on that part and left it as a "disputed issue of fact whether the sexual attack on Susan Box preceded or followed her death."

The next issue was the assistance of counsel. One argument was that his defense attorney at the time let him plead guilty, which bars him from claiming diminished capacity, or that he didn't know what he was doing. The court did not side with Dennis on this argument.

On the issue of Dennis's guilty pleas, Dennis stated that his guilty pleas should be "invalid and must be set aside because (1) they 'were the result of internal compulsion caused by psychiatric disorder rather than a voluntary and intelligent waiver of his constitutional rights' and (2) they did not conform to the California Constitution (art. 1 § 7), requiring a waiver of the right to trial by jury." The Court dismissed this issue as well. Dennis was well aware of what he pled guilty to and was not of diminished capacity.

But here is where the Court failed. Due to the death penalty being "unconstitutional," Dennis's death penalties were reduced to life imprisonment. The kidnapping charges stood, but the kidnapping with robbery charge was dismissed. All judges agreed with the rulings, except Judge McComb, who affirmed in part and disagreed in part. This judge did not agree with modifying the death penalty for the murders. And good for him! These charges should stand; it was supposed to be justice for Susan and Caree, which was denied. With the other 107 or so inmates having their own death sentences changed, would they kill again if they were to be paroled? Only the Parole Board was in charge of that. Governors could overturn Parole Board decisions. Under Governor Pete Wilson, he let most parole decisions go uncontested, although Governor Gray Davis overturned close to three hundred parole board decisions.

Chapter Twenty-Three

On October 13, 1977, Dennis went before the Community Release Board (parole board) accompanied by A. Jarvis, the Department's Representative.

There were no psychiatrists/psychologists attending on behalf of Dennis regarding his treatment at this parole hearing. Due to the lack of information on Dennis's therapy and anything about his "mental outlook," they denied him parole but adds that at the rehearing his physicians are to attend.

On March 10, 1978, Dennis again went before the parole board. W. Higham was Dennis's attorney for this hearing. After going through all of Dennis's offenses, they concluded that "[t]he gravity and brutal viciousness of the violence inherent in the four commitment offenses on four separate victims outweighs the excellent institutional accomplishments, including therapeutic intervention, remorse felt by prisoner for the victims. Panel recognized prisoner's improvement in attitude and behavior... However, the factors considered critical and paramount were the circumstances and the details of the offenses themselves." Dennis was denied parole based on his history of violent behavior, failure to present substantial change for the better, and his mental and emotional state. Amen to this Panel for seeing through all of the crap and remembering the victims.

His next parole hearing was a year later on March 21, 1979. In this hearing Dennis was represented by Attorney Michael R. Snedeker. He submitted quite a lengthy memorandum in support of Dennis being granted parole. This was

Dennis's third appearance before the Board and one that would change so many people's lives, and not for being an outstanding citizen as his attorney and others attest to.

His attorney outlined Dennis's accomplishments and why he needed to be granted parole. His brief to the Board was accompanied by a letter from Edmund Fink, as well as reports from Dennis's therapists. I believe the letter from Edmund had a huge impact. Edmund was successful and educated. He and Dennis connected when Dennis had sent several short stories to the *Kansas City Star*, of which Edmund was the promotion manager. He read his short stories and returned them to Dennis, stating his "writing was good but not professional." What is interesting is why the *Kansas City Star*? He was at San Quentin in California. Dennis had written back to Edmund and that was how their relationship began. Edmund stated he had corresponded with several prisoners around the world.

Of note, Edmund stated, "I have read transcripts of Dennis's trial and am quite familiar with the acts that led to his incarceration. They were horrible. I also know Dennis as he is now, and know him to have transformed himself." Since Edmund didn't know Dennis at the time of his crimes, how did he know that? Did he just go by what Dennis has told him? The transcripts cannot portray how a criminal feels inside. Those are only facts.

The reports from the therapists cover a bit more of what Dennis was feeling at the time of the crimes. They say Dennis felt incompetent as a male but this was "unconscious during the period leading up to the criminal acting out."

Chapter Twenty-Four

Sometime in 1978, was when Dennis had established his close relationship with Edmund. He will play a very critical role in what happened to Dennis. Edmund was born into a very prominent family. His father, Harrison Fink, was a structural engineer, with a bachelor's degree and a master's degree in engineering science management. He was a professor at the University of Kansas during World War II. For over thirty years, he had owned Harrison R. Fink Structural Designing Company, until he retired in 1983. So, Edmund did not want for anything. He attended The Wentworth Military Academy in Lexington, Missouri.

The only difference with Edmund and other boys his age was that Edmund was gay. I am sure being in a military academy was not easy for him. Being gay was not something that you openly spoke of or shown in those days. Being the son of a prominent family probably did not help matters either. I am sure Edmund had his own demons to deal with in life. From what I can tell, Edmund was an only child who never had any children, so the last name of Fink was never carried on.

Edmund succeeded just like his father. He graduated from the University of Kansas with a degree in journalism and advertising. He was the public relations director of the *Kansas City Star* newspaper. He retired from there in 1977. After he retired from the newspaper, he went on to become a professor teaching the Principles of Advertising class at three different colleges in the Kansas City area.

One thing Edmund was an avid lover of was ice-skating. According to his obituary, he was on the teaching staff of the Foxhill Skating Arena in Prairie Village, Kansas, as well as a member of the Kansas City Figure Skating Club. He was also associated with the Ice Capades promotional staff. So, it begs you to wonder how in the world did Edmund get mixed up with Dennis?

At some point in their relationship, Edmund had adopted Dennis as his son. Was this all done because he didn't have any children or because he was in love with Dennis? Only Edmund knows. It is hard to understand why Edmund had anything to do with Dennis to begin with. A lot of people have the "second chances" mentality, and I guess Dennis would be a candidate from being such a "model" prisoner, but people forgot about the victims. What about them? Did Edmund ever think about that?

For example, there was a case in Missouri where a young woman in her early twenties killed the father of a two-year-old after she hit them head on in a collision due to her drinking and driving. The father was killed, and the two-year-old miraculously survived. The woman went to her hearing after more than a year and a half of being out on bail and was sentenced to four months in prison. FOUR months! That is what you get now days for drinking and driving and killing someone. Drug dealers get more time than that.

What blows my mind is that the family of the woman felt bad she was going to go to prison for four months, but no one thinks about the child and that now she is without her father. What about her? She got this very light sentence because an abundance of people testified that the woman was a "good person." Plus, it doesn't hurt when you have a well-paid attorney. Once again, what about the victim?

This woman didn't learn her lesson. She has total disregard for other people, including her family. I doubt she even thinks about what she did, or that this little girl is now fatherless. She has no idea what it is to lose someone you love, if she had, maybe she would be a little more human. Say what you want, but this woman is a murderer, plain and simple.

Chapter Twenty-Five

On Wednesday, March 21, 1979, Dennis attended his third parole hearing. His previous hearings from 1974-1978 were denied. Keep in mind it's only been a year since the last hearing where he was denied parole. But at this hearing, things would certainly be different. Once again, he was represented by Michael Snedeker. He had prepared a memorandum to present to the Board. He gave a brief rundown of Dennis's crimes and then went on to list all of the things Dennis had accomplished. With regard to remorse, he stated, "Feelings of remorse nearly overwhelmed him for years after the murder...Mr. Stanworth's real problem has not been to understand the nature and enormity of his crimes, but rather to learn to live with himself in full knowledge of their magnitude." This would be one of those times you hope that the murderer sees the faces of these girls in his dreams every night. It is not Christian-like, but it is hard not to wish ill will to him for what he had done. In reading a lot of these documents, I almost get the feeling that people felt sorry for him because he was locked up and he was such a great guy. The Parole Board officers for this hearing were Presiding Member N.A. (Chad) Chaderjian; Ralph Pizzaro, Member of the Community Release Board; and Mrs. Ruth Rushen, Vice-Chairman of the Community Release Board. Also present from the State of California was William Bartlett from the Contra Costa County District Attorney's Office. The beginning of the hearing just went over all of his offenses and what was going on in his life at that time. As stated earlier,

Dennis still had the urge to rape and wanted to discuss it with his wife, where they came to an agreement that they would have sex. But as time went on, this didn't resolve his urges to rape women, so he kept away from his wife so she didn't know that he still had the urges.

Mrs. Rushen addressed Dennis's accomplishments after getting off death row. In 1977 he was assigned to horticulture, and it was stated that his attitude and work habits were "excellent." Dennis added that he also obtained a one-year certificate in computer programming. She then moved on to his psychiatric evaluations. The first evaluation was done by Dr. R.S. Rood. He stated in his 1974 report that, "(i)f it were not for the homicide, he (Dennis) could be judged a mentally disordered sex offender." The next report to be addressed was from Dr. H.D. Ferber, Staff Psychologist, and approved by L. Loughlin, Chief Psychiatrist. His diagnosis was Dennis had "sexual deviation with sadomasochistic tendencies, improved." Basically the doctors, as well as Dennis, had requested ongoing therapy "(i)n order to consolidate his gains."

Another report was done in 1976 by Dr. Ferber, wherein he stated that Dennis "(h)as been a highly motivated participant in individual therapy. He is coming to grips with many of his major difficulties and is expected to continue to do so in the future."

Then in another report in 1977 by Dr. Ferber basically summed up that Dennis could recognize his destructive patterns and work through them. He recommended that Dennis be offered parole within the next two to three years.

In a report dated February 23, 1979, Dr. LG. Nuernberger, staff psychologist, recommended parole for Dennis as he had then become more independent and had the capacity to accept responsibility for his actions, as well as his advances in his treatment.

Presiding Member Pizzaro took over the last phase of the hearing dealing with his parole release plans. At the time an educational fund of $12,000 was set up for Dennis by Edmund Fink, as well as $3,000 in Dennis' savings from working in the prison and also selling his carpentry work. These things brought quite a bit of weight in this hearing. It showed that Dennis did have plans. Mr. Pizzaro addresses Dennis's personal life with regards to his ex-wife (Pamela) and the kids. Dennis stated the kids had no contact with him since he was imprisoned, and that the only way he knows what's going on with them is when the kids saw his mom and dad since they are still their grandparents. Dennis stated he was visited by his mom and dad, his brothers, and his M-2 sponsor. So, his family didn't abandon him when he was in prison. He also stated that Edmund Fink continued to write to him. At some point in Dennis's incarceration, he had met a woman and they had planned on marrying, but he said he called it off because it wouldn't make sense to be married to someone on the outside. He had met her while she was on tour of the prison.

Further on into the hearing, Dennis stated that he would like to pursue something in psychology due to what he has learned about himself, and he felt he could help children with his same issues. What in the world? What parent would allow a person like Dennis counsel their children? I certainly wouldn't. If it didn't take much for him to kill two teenagers; what's to say he wouldn't suddenly get the urge during a session? Is he going to stop that session in order to call someone or get away from the situation? I find it hard to believe he would.

Dennis's attorney also submitted a letter from Dr. James Vaughan, who was the staff psychologist, dated May 29, 1974. It stated Dennis had led a double life when these crimes occurred, being that he was the member of church and leader but had a "fantasy life of turmoil and intense self-hatred." Since he was always told to be a "good boy," he basically hid those feelings and until the crimes had never acted out in that sort of way. This letter was five years before his actual parole date and the doctor had stated that Dennis would "have excellent prospects for good adjustment back in the community."

The end result of this hearing was Dennis was paroled. This was based on the following factors: lack of prior serious criminal history, excellent work record, receiving an associate of arts degree and a certificate in data processing, participation in therapy, no infractions in the last ten years, no psychiatric con-tradictions, and his parole plans regarding education and the fact that he had a significant amount in his savings account.

Chapter Twenty-Six

The total time Dennis was sentenced to prison for was seventeen years for the first-degree murder of Susan Box; two years for the personal use of a firearm and the other crimes that he had admitted to; seven years for the murder of Caree; three years for forcible rape; eighteen months for the oral copulation of Patricia Scott, giving him a total of thirty years and six months. They went on to give him credit for post-conviction behavior with two to three months for each year that he served on death row, four months for each year after leaving death row, totaling forty-two months.

So, in total he was sentenced to twenty-three years, four months, and nine days for a parole release on April 16, 1990. Think about that for a second. A *total* of roughly twenty-three and a half years for two murders and the rape and kidnapping of six women. There was no justice for these women, especially Susan and Caree. The last few minutes of their lives were the face of a monster. Although Caree lived beyond that day, she was comatose and never regained consciousness, so I feel she was dead the same time Susan was. But, then to go on and rape Susan after she died? That must be one of the most heinous acts a human being can ever do to another, not to mention a fifteen-year-old.

While Dennis was in prison for his remaining years, he was quite active in the prison system. I found a San Quentin internal newspaper called the *San Quentin News* dated Friday, June 30, 1981, in which Dennis speaks of his hobbies.

He stated he has been, "hobbying off and on for the last eight of his fourteen years" at San Quentin. He stated that many people think that the hobby program is nothing but play. When asked Dennis stated, "On the contrary, the hobbyist must learn to think, plan, and take responsibility for his own success. Besides the skills I've learned in working the crafts—and I've tried my hand in most all of them—I've also had to develop a good business sense. I have to know what sells and I have to know what's going to cost me to make the items."

On another San Quentin newsletter dated July 10, 1981, Dennis was featured in that he had built a forty-two-foot catamaran model. It stated this was a scale model to one that he would build when he returns to the streets. Dennis stated, "I've loved boats since I was a small boy, and have wanted a boat all my life... I have studied boat design and I'm self-taught (while here at SQ) on how to build and design boats. The model was a learning experience so I'd know what changes will be needed on the full size 'cat.'"

The prison actually launched this catamaran, named the *GypSea*, on a pond at Coyote Park. It was marveled by a few people and one man had said it would be even more beautiful if it had been bigger and on the bay with him. I don't doubt that it was beautiful; I don't think there's any question as to Dennis's talents when it came to carpentry and the like. It's just hard to give praise to someone so evil. They actually sent the model back to Dennis's wife at the time.

Dennis was involved in a lot of activities and jobs in prison but was also involved in a lot of court hearings and arguments about his rights. He and his attorney filed motion after motion while he was in prison, even up to a few years before he was paroled.

Chapter Twenty-Seven

In 1982, the warden at San Quentin had wanted Dennis moved to a less secure facility in what they call the dorms. Instead of taking that offer, Dennis fought them to stay on the farm at San Quentin. He stated this was due to his close relationships with his family, and most of all, Edmund. I just have a hard time understanding their relationship. I do wonder if it had to do with Edmund's sexuality, or even Dennis's due to his hatred of women at the time of his offenses. Edmund had written a letter dated September 8, 1982, to Charles Bishop of the San Quentin Prison Law Office regarding Dennis wanting to stay where he was.

The letterhead of this letter states Edmund was an Advertising Education Consultant with an address in Kansas City, Missouri, so he had not made a move to California as of that time. He stated in the letter that he was an important role model in Dennis's life, and due to where he was incarcerated, Edmund could easily visit him since it was in San Francisco and stated the reason why it was convenient to keep him there. One thing I found interesting is regarding the adoption of Dennis; in his letter Edmund stated, "I legally adopted Dennis several years ago at my lawyer's suggestion to clarify some provisions of my will." There was a provision in his will that a portion of his assets goes to schools, so in order to work around that he needed to adopt Dennis. Edmund stated he had been going out to see Dennis every other month for the last five years. This was a lot of money spent on the likes of Dennis. The major question I have is why? Why would such a successful and educated man take on the responsibility of taking care of Dennis, a murderer and rapist? Edmund concluded his letter with "I sincerely believe it is in the interest of the California prison system to nurture this relationship between Dennis and myself and not arbitrarily relocate him where it will be a severe hardship for us to maintain personal contact."

Along with Edmund's letter was numerous correspondence from Dennis as well as statements from others within the prison that Dennis had worked with, all stating it would be detrimental to their departments and Dennis if they decided to move him to another facility. All of them wrote nothing but good things about him and how excellent he was as a student and as a person overall.

Dennis stated in his letter that his mother and father visited him regularly. According to his timeline in the letter, these are all of the things he has accomplished since he went into the prison system: High school education courses, was part of the "Honor Condemned Row Unit," hobby program, worked as a clerk in the hospital, classes in Vocational Electronics Data Processing, obtained an associate's degree from the College of Marin, was approved by Alpha Gamma Sigma society to be a member from the College of Marin, worked in the Industries Warehouse as a clerk, started Vocational Landscape Gardening program, and a clerk for the handicraft program. All of this sounds impressive, doesn't it, if you overlook his crimes.

He also states, "In summary, except for a brief period of violent behavior that occurred (sic) over a brief period of time at age twenty-two and twenty-three during the years of 1965 and 1966, which brought me to San Quentin, the behavioral pattern I hope I have demonstrated here is who I am. I behave well simply because it has always been in my self-interest to do so and that is how I get along best in life. I enjoy and receive great pleasure from how I am."

I just have a hard time with this statement. Did he love himself when he killed Susan and Caree? There is no way of knowing the answer to this question. Although Dennis was a remorseful person, what was he remorseful of exactly?

In the end he made a very convincing case, and he stayed at the farm in San Quentin. When you read the correspondence from Dennis, he sounds very educated, knows what his rights are, and is confident in what he is presenting.

How does a killer who was on death row make it this far within the prison system and be hailed as an upstanding prisoner? Should he be more apt to be released because of these accomplishments? Once again, the victims are forgotten. It's about what Dennis has done in prison, when he is surrounded by others and has certain restraints, but no one thinks about the "what ifs" if Dennis is going to be released. Along with the brief is breakdown in chronological order of Dennis's time in the prison system. It stated that in 1968 he did have an infraction with littering the tier with water and trash and received fifteen days cell study and thirty days loss of a privilege-cell study. That makes no sense, but that was his punishment. That was his only infraction while he was incarcerated.

Chapter Twenty-Eight

Regarding the legal issues of his case, Dennis's final appeal was in December 1982. This was to appeal Dennis' sentence under the new sentencing computation of the Determinate Sentencing Law (DSL) instead of the Indeterminate Sentence Law (ISL). He wanted his sentence given by the Parole Board to be determined under the ISL and not the stricter DSL guidelines.

Under the ISL, the parole board could consider the inmates' individual characteristics, such as time spent and the accomplishments they had made while in prison. The Board had the discretion to make certain adjustments in a sentence and the inmate was entitled to release. Under the DSL, it was mandatory that the Board make adjustments to sentences based upon certain crimes, whether it be more time or less time. The DSL took on the view that the purpose of imprisonment is for punishment and there should be no discretion given to the Board. The sentences were set to a certain amount of time based on the severity of the crime. Under DSL you were only credited a max of one fourth of the time sentenced, and with a maximum of four months per year. His argument is not his date of release but if the new law is a detriment to him. He did not get a parole hearing in between the original ISL guidelines and when the DSL was enacted, and he should be sentenced under the ISL rules.

In summary, the Court found that Dennis's computation of time should be under both sets of laws. It really didn't make a difference; he still spent twenty-four years in prison. He was released back into society in 1990 with supervision.

I wanted to find out more about Dennis, so I spoke with Dennis's Appellant Attorney, Michael Snedeker. Mr. Snedeker stated that Dennis was "very remorseful" for what he did. Remorseful or not, his crimes were heinous.

To find out more about Edmund's role in this, Mr. Snedeker stated that Dennis had questioned his sexuality. Maybe that was why Dennis and Edmund bonded. He stated that when Dennis was paroled, Dennis and Edmund "had opened a business together across the river from Martinez." I was unable to find any records to substantiate this statement. He may have been confused with Dennis Jr., who does own a business in Nevada City, California. Mr. Snedeker also stated that Dennis had sent him a few cards after he got out of prison, but stopped sending them after a while and hadn't heard from him in years.

At some point while living in California, Edmund had bought a house in a golf course community in Vallejo, California. Dennis also lived there. I visited this home, and I have to tell you, they were not struggling by any means. While he was in California, Edmund was still involved in dance and the arts. He played the character Herr Drosselemeyer in Tchaikovsky's *The Nutcracker* with the Benicia Ballet for eleven seasons. He also had the talent for figure drawing, which is basically drawing from a live model. He had some of his drawings on display in some of the galleries around the San Francisco area, but it didn't pan into anything that successful.

This home in Vallejo would prove to be a house of evil.

Chapter Twenty-Nine

Sometime after Dennis's release from prison, he met Cecile "Cissy" Bonaudi. Cecile was from Utah, same as Dennis. She didn't have any children of her own but had three nephews whom she loved very much. Cecile was also Mormon like Dennis, so they had that in common. She also had a love of the arts.

I was able to speak with one of Cissy's nephews who stated that Cissy made a living by playing poker at the casinos and did very well for herself. If you can make a living doing that, then you must be pretty darn good. This is where Dennis and Cecile crossed paths. It's never been established whether Cecile knew of Dennis's past or not. If she did, she must not have cared because they ended up getting married, although she never publicly changed her last name to Stanworth. Who would blame her? I wouldn't either.

This begs the question of whether or not Dennis questioned his sexuality; if he had, then why be with a woman? Her family also conveyed that she and Edmund did not get along at first, but at some point she put that aside because she stayed with Dennis and Edmund for many years. All three of them lived together. Awkward? I would say so. Did she question the adoption of Dennis by Edmund? I can't seem to wrap my head around that, but I am not privy to the information of the adoption since adoption records are sealed and I couldn't get a hold of Dennis's biological children.

One of the neighbors I spoke with said that she would see Cecile with Dennis and "her father," and that they seemed like very nice people. Larry Collison's widow stated she and her daughter (from another marriage) had gone to this golf course neighborhood warning people of Dennis's past and were handing out flyers to the neighbors. I guess it didn't really make an impact because one of Dennis's neighbors, Irving Vanderberg stated, "I figured he had paid for his mistakes according to the law."

Dennis would stay dormant, so to say, for twenty-five years, until the evil inside him peaked its head once again.

Chapter Thirty

Dennis's mom, "Nellie Belle," as she was called, lived close to Dennis while he was in California. Dennis's father passed away in 2002, so Nellie moved to a nearby mobile home park in Vallejo to be closer to him. Dennis's brother, Paul, still lived in Utah, and his brother, Larry, had already passed away from cirrhosis of the liver, so Dennis was all she had near her. I drove through this park and it was very neat, well kept, and looked like a pretty quiet area, and definitely away from the hustle and bustle of the city. There were a lot of flowers around the neighborhood in pots put on their decks and railings. It was very comforting, and I could imagine Nellie just sitting on her porch enjoying all of them. Thirl was the one to plant flowers and Nellie planted tomatoes.

I have been in contact with one of the grandchildren of Nellie and Thirl, and listening to them speak of these two as grandparents was every grandkid's wish, at least mine anyway. I will refer to their grandchild as "they," so it keeps their identity even more private. The Stanworth family does not deserve cruel punishment and be labeled because of the monstrous acts of one family member. There was no one to blame for these acts except Dennis. Could a few people who surrounded Dennis during that time see the warning signs? Absolutely! But they did nothing about it. I hate to put blame on anyone, but I think if Pamela at the time would have been more aware of Dennis's changing persona, some things may have been avoided. I have a hard time understanding how she didn't do anything when he had told her he tried to kidnap someone, but I wasn't there and I'm not her. I would have liked to have gotten more from her side but since I didn't receive a response, I will have to go with what Dennis and the court records say.

Nellie was remembered as a happy person who loved to laugh a lot, with a "little snort thrown in." She loved to sing and with most sentences she seemed to sing rather than speak them. That is truly a sign of happiness. Nellie had worked for one of the hospitals in Pinole as a supply admin. She was in charge of ordering supplies the hospital needed. Everyone at the hospital loved her and told the family such they would visit the hospital on occasions.

They fondly remember that their grandparents' car glove box was always full of Brach's candies, and they were always allowed to take a couple. One thing my son can depend on regarding his grandparents (my parents) is there is always chocolate in the house. My dad certainly cannot live without chocolate.

Something that tickles me is every morning Nellie and Thirl would go to the park. While Nellie was walking around the park, Thirl would wait in the car eating donut holes. I think this is true love; it's something that they do together, and it belongs to only them, and no one else can share that with them.

In other correspondence, it was mentioned that the boys had a "rift" with Thirl, but other family members don't remember the boys and Thirl ever getting in an argument or having hatred toward each other. Maybe that was just something in Dennis's mind to try to explain why he was the way he was. Dennis had mentioned that he was traumatized from an incident where his father had killed a squirrel in front of him. So, because your dad killed an animal in front of you, you decided that is one of the reasons you were messed up? That squirrel could have been dinner. I don't buy this excuse one bit. All of us have gone through something traumatizing, just maybe some more than others, but that doesn't make them become a rapist and murderer. I feel he tried to explain his behavior by placing the blame on someone else. Dennis was the one who committed the crimes, not his family. They were not standing there with a gun to Dennis's head; he made the wrong choices of his own doing.

Dennis's brother, Larry, had passed away in 1995 from long-term alcohol abuse, which some in his family correlate to him living with the guilt of Dennis's crimes. This shows you that there are more victims than just the victims of the crime itself. Victims within the family of the monster who committed the crimes can be victimized just as much. Larry was around twelve to thirteen years of age at the time of the crimes. He was musically talented and knew how to play a few instruments, including the piano and organ. Family members remember he would play the piano and the organ at the same time they visited. After high school, Larry went into the Air Force and played the trumpet since the field he wanted to go in was not available. One thing that the family remembers is that Larry was always afraid that the Stanworth name would be in the news again, and unfortunately that is what happened.

Dennis's other brother, Paul, had lived in Nevada, so Dennis was Nellie's closest child after Thirl died. From what others say, he took pretty good care of her, taking her to doctor's appointments and making sure she took her medicines, things you would do for an elderly parent.

Sometime around August 2012, Dennis had taken Nellie away from her home to put her in an assisted living facility. Nellie's neighbor from the mobile home park stated Nellie returned shortly after that, complaining about her living situation. A few months later, Dennis came again to pick up Nellie, and Dennis told the neighbor that he was taking her to live with her sister, and they did not see her again after that. So, what happened to Nellie?

Chapter Thirty-One

One January 9, 2013, Vallejo Police Department dispatch received a call from a seventy-year-old gentleman who had admitted to killing his mother, saying he "couldn't live with himself anymore." This caller was none other than Dennis. The ultimate betrayal of killing your own mother. After everything Nellie had done for Dennis, this is how he repaid her. It is very heartbreaking to read what he did to his mother.

According to the coroner's report from Solano County, Dennis stated his mother had "lived long enough." Nellie was ninety years old at the time but relatively healthy. Dennis had confessed that he hit Nellie over the head with a brick, preceded to slit her throat, and throw her in a garbage can with dirt, lyme, and chlorine on top of her. At this point there was no telling what her time/date of death was since it had been months before Dennis reported it, but the reports put it on or about November 6, 2012.

It's difficult to read the report, but it shows how evil Dennis was. The coroner "found the deceased in a plastic trash can on the side of the house. I emptied the trashcan to find the deceased placed in the trash can headfirst, toward the bottom of the trashcan. The decedent's arms appeared to be at her side. It appeared the decedent had a blanket wrapped on her torso and had pants on. The decedent also had a plastic bucket over her head, with a dent in it. The body was in poor condition showing signs of decomposition."

Cause of death was noted to be blunt force trauma to the head and the slash to her throat. They found two lacerations to her head, which most likely came from hitting her with a brick. She had a ¾" deep laceration to her abdominal wall. Additionally it was noted she was wearing blue pants and three shirts. Dennis had placed her in a blue tarp with a "knitted afghan/shawl that is partially wrapped around her head and shoulders." This statement is heartbreaking due to the fact that most times older ladies are the ones who knit and crochet, so I would guess it was one she had done herself, but that's just speculation on my part.

She was wearing a necklace with some sort of beads, which had been broken when Dennis cut into her throat, and some of the beads were embedded into the wound. The laceration to her throat was roughly four inches across and one inch deep.

From the toxicology report, she was taking the medication Paxil, which is used for depression, although it could be used for other disorders as well. Considering her life at that time, it's not too farfetched to assume it's for depression. The only family she had left was Paul and Dennis. There was also a trace amount of morphine. I was told that Nellie was in a lot of back pain, so she may have taken some sort of pain killer.

Nellie was ninety years old and would have lived longer had it not been for Dennis. The only things that contributed to her death were what Dennis did. There was nothing naturally wrong with her. She may have lived long enough according to Dennis, but she was a very healthy ninety-year-old. He ultimately stole from her whatever good times she had left to enjoy.

One family remember stated, "About a month before I knew she had died, I had a dream about her where she came to me in an empty parking garage and was climbing up and down the stairs and flying around in a little go cart thing saying look how amazing it is I can do all of this and I am in no pain at all... I can run and jump and climb, I feel amazing. I now have spent the last eight years wondering if she had already died, just none of us knew it yet. And, perhaps she really did communicate with me in my dreams that I shouldn't worry, that she is okay now." I do believe things like this happening where you feel a loved one has spoken to you in the afterlife, so to say.

I remember my own instance where my late husband had died in a freak accident and the night he died, while I was crying trying to close my eyes to get some sort of sleep, I heard him say, "I'm sorry, honey." That is what we always called each other. It was clear as day to me, and I knew he meant it. He did not mean to leave me so early, but God had other plans.

This family member went on to say that after Dennis got out of prison and was taken care of by Edmund, "I don't know how he managed to have that type of fortune or luck fall into his lap like that... It all just doesn't seem like the way karma is supposed to work..." One of the greatest fears of the family was "Dennis would put the Stanworth name back in the media, and we would all have to go through all of the things that we already had to go through..." I would completely agree with her. How does someone come across good fortune when they don't deserve to live in happiness after stealing the happiness from so many others?

Nellie's family, the ones who had nothing to do with Dennis, stated that their hearts go out to the families of the victims and they are "so very sad and sorry." The family of the criminals are also banished from society and the media makes sure that happens. It is amazing when I hear of the victim's family forgive the perpetrator. It is not the family's fault; it is the criminal's fault. Coming from the victim's side, I am sure it's hard not to blame someone in the family.

Chapter Thirty-Two

Dennis was charged with murder with prior murder conviction, which carries the death penalty, and taken to the Vallejo Police Department to await his arraignment, which is the first hearing to decide what to do with him and how to proceed with the charges. This was his third time of being in front of a jury to be judged and possibly receive the death penalty. But this time he was seventy years old. We know he wouldn't be given the needle; he would most certainly die before then. Most of the time people sit on death row for well over ten years, so he would most likely die in prison. Do you consider this justice?

After hearing of Dennis's crime, Susan's sisters had written to the district attorney in which they wrote, "A couple of years ago my family found that Dennis Stanworth was out of prison, he had been paroled after being sentenced to the death penalty for killing Susan and her friend, Carrie. Imagine my family's shock first of all by him being paroled, out of prison and then living about forty-five minutes from our homes. Our family wasn't even notified that he was being considered to be paroled. Aren't the victim's families supposed to be notified...I feel that Susan and her friend, Carrie, died and their killer was set free. Where is justice?" I completely agree with this statement. Where was the justice? He only spent twenty-three years in prison for killing two innocent teenage girls, and he was out to enjoy freedom and with the resources he had with Edmund he lived a pretty good life.

His first hearing was on January 11, 2013, at which time it was decided Dennis would remain in jail and a public defender would be tentatively appointed. Edmund was still in Dennis's life, so I don't understand why he wouldn't have outside counsel. Edmund certainly had the money. Maybe this time Edmund would not look past Dennis's crimes; after all, this time it affected Edmund as well. I am sure he knew Nellie very well at this point, not to mention that she was stuffed into a garbage can right next to his house for months and no one knew about it. But did they?

Dennis was represented by Chief Public Defender Oscar Bobrow. Dennis was shackled to a wheelchair. Deputy District Attorney Karen Jensen stated, "He was emotional but said he was able to stand and walk." In the middle of the hearing, Dennis blurted out, "I want to plead guilty to all charges. I admit everything and this is the third time." Considering Dennis's mental state, I have conflicting feelings about him, due to his age. The struggle I had with this book is you almost feel sorry for him, but you have to keep in mind all of the other crimes he committed, especially to two fifteen-year-old girls.

In the end the Court continued this hearing until January 18, 2013, so there would be time for Dennis to get a public defender. At this hearing, attorney Lesli Caldwell appeared from the Public Defender's Office on Dennis's behalf but withdrew from the case due to a conflict with her availability. The Court had to continue the case again until February 21, 2013. After every hearing Dennis would be taken back to the Solano County jail, where he sat until he was officially charged and possibly sent back to San Quentin, his old stomping grounds. The only person left on death row from his era was Charles Manson. Imagine Dennis going back and hanging out with Charles Manson. I would like to say that Dennis was more evil because his crimes were done by his own hands.

Chapter Thirty-Three

Another hearing was held on February 21, 2013, and ended very differently. I believe due to his age the Prosecution announced they would not seek the death penalty. I guess for me it would have been justice just to have them say he was sentenced to death; it has a better ring to it than he's already going to die in prison, so why seek it. The hearing was continued so the prosecution and the public defender could prepare for the case to be heard in court.

On June 18, 2013, Thomas Barrett of the Public Defender's Conflict office requested a continuance because "counsel needs additional time to investigate and prepare." Mr. Barrett had just started with the Conflict Office on May 28, 2013, so he would need more time. In this request it mentioned Dennis experiencing a stroke in January 2012. I had not been given any information pertaining to this. Can a stroke cause you to have a poor sense of judgment and end with you killing your mother? I am sure that argument will be made at some point. They started to question his "mental state and cognition."

This case was just hearing after hearing and continuance after continuance. Another hearing was held on August 16, 2013, and this was when Dennis pled not guilty and the case will go to trial. A hearing held on November 21, 2013, the Court decided that Dennis needed to be evaluated by Dr.'s Janice Nakagawa, Ph.D., and Stephen Pittavino, Ph.D. as to Dennis's mental competence to "understand the nature and purpose of the proceedings taken against him;

cooperate in a rational manner with counsel in presenting a defense; and prepare and conduct his own defense in a rational manner without counsel." They were also to address if antipsychotic medication will help him in his defense, voluntarily or involuntary taken. Dr. Pittavaino noted he observed Dennis's emotional stability. He stated, "At certain moments the defendant suddenly and unexpectedly becomes tearful, only to just as suddenly re-compose himself." They contribute this to a pseudo effect and it as "organically related." In layman's terms, this means he just has outbursts of emotions due to the strokes he had in the past. Could some of this be related to the situation he was in? According to the doctors, Dennis was basically mentally gone and could not become competent no matter the treatment he received.

The next hearing was scheduled for December 19, 2013, after the doctors had the opportunity to evaluate him.

Dennis had a neurological evaluation done on December 13, 2013, and it was determined by Dr. Dale Watson that "Mr. Stanworth has previously been diagnosed with probable Alzheimer's Dementia and is status-post cerebral vascular accident. (CVA)." A CT scan was performed on January 9, 2012, at which time it was noted that Dennis had "age-related cerebral atrophy with compensatory volume loss slightly greater than expected for the patient's age." There was evidence that Dennis, at some point in the past, had suffered a stroke.

At the hearing on December 19, 2013, the prosecutor, Karen Jensen, requested a jury trial to determine if the jury felt Dennis was competent, which was set for March 10, 2014.

In late January, early February 2014, Dennis's health had deteriorated to the point that the Solano County Sheriff's Office had requested of the court that Dennis be moved to the California Medical Facility (CMF) of the state prison in Vacaville, California. In a request to the Court dated February 7, 2014, Ramona Margherio, attorney for the Solano County Sheriff's Office, stated that Dennis "presents a serious custodial challenge due to his continually escalating medical needs that require ongoing skilled and non-skilled custodial medical care beyond the level of care able to be provided by the jail." They believed he was only going to deteriorate more and would require better care than what they could provide.

On April 21, 2014, the Court and the Prosecution agreed to transfer Dennis to the Napa State Hospital and admitted him to the hospital's Trial Competency

Restoration Program, and that the Sheriff's Office delivered him to the facility so he could be provided the care he needed. It was also ordered that antipsychotic drugs be administered involuntarily to Dennis as his doctor's saw fit.

Mr. Barrett advised the Court on May 29, 2014, that Dennis had yet to be transferred to the medical facility. Throughout the time from the Court order to Mr. Barrett's petition to the Court, he had called the Public Information Officer of the Sheriff's Department but could not get in touch with anyone. They couldn't get any sort of confirmation that Dennis was still at the CMF. Mr. Barrett had even looked through Vinelink online (which tells you where people are in the prison system across the United States) and there was no record of where Dennis was at the time. So, not even his attorney, Cecile, or Edmund could find out where he was. Cecile and Edmund were denied contact once Dennis was put into the CMF.

When Mr. Barrett finally spoke with the attorney of the Sheriff's Department, Ms. Margherio, she told him it showed Dennis was still at the CMF, but she had no confirmation. He brought to her attention the Court's decision that Dennis was to be moved to the Napa State Hospital due to his deteriorating health and he should have been transferred. Ms. Margherio said it would be very soon when he would be moved but could not give a definite date.

Since Dennis had still not been moved, Mr. Barrett had no other choice but to petition the Court to order the sheriff's office to appear and explain why Dennis had not yet been moved. He had requested a hearing date of June 13, 2014, at which time an official hearing on the matter would be held on July 25, 2014. This whole time Dennis was deteriorating mentally and psychically. Prior to this June 25 hearing, the judge had ruled they would not have the hearing on June 13, 2014, and he was to be placed immediately into Napa State Hospital, which finally took place on July 8, 2014.

<h1 style="text-align:center">Chapter Thirty-Four</h1>

I won't go through each and every court matter that was brought forth during the months that followed because there are so many, and it's tedious going back and forth between the hospital, the Prosecutor, the Public Defender's office, and the Guardian. Basically, it came down to Dennis not being able to be cared for at Napa State Hospital anymore because it was determined there was no hope of him ever being competent to stand trial and help in his own defense. Due to this decision, Dennis needed to be moved to another facility, and that was when a guardian was assigned to his case.

The guardian for Dennis's case requested on August 29, 2014, that Dennis be evaluated by Dr. Paul Ryfa, who was a Conservatorship Investigator for Solano County. Dr. Ryfa evaluated Dennis on September 24, 2014.

The diagnosis the doctors had opined prior to this appointment was "Antisocial Personality Disorder, Alzheimer's disease, Major Neurocognitive Disorder due to Multiple Etiologies with behavioral disturbance, Major Vascular Neurocognitive disorder with behavioral disturbance." So, Dennis pretty much had a behavior problem, no surprise there. I guess this part of him never subsided once he got out of prison. And honestly, who would be able to tell and deal with it anyway? For the most part, his only close family/friends were Cecile and Edmund, and I would bet that both of them protected him. Due to Edmund's sexuality and his closeness with Dennis, it doesn't surprise me if he protected

Dennis, but if Cecile did, I do not understand that. She had to feel some sort of sympathy, if not at least empathy, for the women he hurt in his life, regardless of whether or not "he paid his dues." I can't imagine her trying to protect him if she knew he killed his mother, since it happened right in front of her, so to speak.

It is stated in Dr. Ryfa's report that the information he used for this evaluation was from medical records, interviews with staff, an interview with Cecile, and he had also interviewed Dennis. He stated Dennis had a history of antisocial personality disorder and violence toward women and outlined Dennis's crimes.

In reading the doctor's report, there is a lot of conflicting information between what was initially reported and the information he was given by Cecile. He was told that after prison, "Dennis attended Solano Community College where he met Cecile and Edmund Fink." We know that is not true. So, is the doctor mistaken or was Cecile hiding the way Edmund and Dennis met? She stated they all became friends and Edmund invited her and Dennis to come and live with him. I also know that is not true. According to Dennis's Appellant Attorney, Mr. Snedeker, Edmund and Dennis had plans to open up a business when Dennis had gotten out of prison. I am sure Edmund had Dennis move in with him as soon as he got out of prison. Dennis already had degrees while he was in prison; why would he go to college on the outside? The inner personal relationships these three had are hard to understand.

According to Cecile, once Dennis got out of prison, he had taken on a few small jobs working in a boatyard and painting houses, as well as helping at the Senior Center in Vallejo, California.

She also stated that he had suffered a stroke in 2000, and again after he was in jail in 2013, and felt after this last stroke he became significantly impaired and showed signs of dementia. I know from personal experience and stories from other friends who experienced it that dementia itself can be very hard to live with from the patient's point of view as well as the family. Imagine not being able to remember things, or for example, putting your keys in the refrigerator and forgetting where you put them. Calling your family in the middle of the night asking them why they haven't been fed because they think it's the daytime but it was actually 1:00 A.M. When you think about it, wouldn't that be some sort of mental torture? So, is Dennis experiencing karma, and ultimate revenge for what he did in his past?

When Dennis was interviewed, he appeared well dressed but was in a wheelchair and would stare at the wall most of the time and appeared confused. He stated, "Mr. Stanworth has limited, if any, speech, and at the time of my interview he was unable to answer any of my questions. He is unable to make his needs known." He stated that when Dennis was admitted to Napa State Hospital, he "began screaming, apparently out of some paranoid belief. He was, however, able to function in all other areas. In the past few months, however, he has lost much of his ability to care for himself. Dr Coburn stated he did not expect Mr. Stanworth to live beyond the next twelve months, given his very rapid decline in functioning."

Cecile was aware of the fragile state that Dennis was in and requested the court that she be able to take care of him. The Court had denied this request because of the constant care Dennis would need, and they felt she would not provide him with everything he needs. She felt, "Dennis would be better off dying in his home than in the hospital." Looking at Dennis from his court hearing, he was not a small guy. Cecile was not tiny by any means, but I don't believe she would have been able to take care of him with all of the needs he had. His daily living needs required "a gurney style wheelchair and Hoyer lift. He is unable to feed himself or operate his wheelchair. He requires assistance in all areas of functioning, including dressing, bathing, feeding, turning to prevent bedsores, toileting, and taking medications. He requires adult diapers and is unable to change himself." I don't know about you, but that is a lot for a wife to carry, regardless of how much you love them. Cecile was not healthy either. She was using medicinal marijuana during that time for chronic pain.

One thing that brings the question is why isn't Edmund also interviewed? He had known Dennis longer than anyone, including most of his family. He had been married twice before Cecile, but not for any significant length of time, and one marriage was while he was incarcerated.

Of interesting note in this report, Dennis had told the doctor that he lived in American Canyon with his mother until 2012, he killed her in 2013, was arrested, and he can't go back to his home, so he was homeless. This was listed under Living Arrangements prior to hospitalization. This is interesting because it would seem that Dennis had lived with Nellie, took her to his home, killed her, and then Edmund and Cecile had asked him not to return to the residence. Makes you wonder, did that mean they knew what Dennis had done? Had Dennis admitted to it? And if so, why didn't they do anything? Unfortunately that is a question that will not be answered.

Dr. Ryfa went on to say that Dr. Coburn also stated that it would be "inhumane to attempt to move Mr. Stanworth from the hospital setting as the transfer to a different environment which has less nursing staff who don't know his condition well enough would probably result in his passing." Inhumane? Wasn't it inhumane to do what he did to all of those women, and take the lives of two innocent teenage girls? I guess some people are more forgiving than others and believe everyone has a right to life, no matter their past. That is something that some, like me, cannot do.

I know all will be judged before God and that is the ultimate price you will pay, but why should someone so evil be given a chance at life on this earth and breathe the same air we breathe when they took the breath of others? I do have some empathy for those who take the life of someone else because of what that person has done to them, such as those who rape, child molesters, or even those who murder persons who killed a member of their family by the perpetrators acts of stupidity and cruelty. It is hard to have any empathy for someone that is just plain evil.

The findings of Dr. Ryfa's report is that Dennis was "gravely disabled as a result of mental illness. He shall be denied the right to refuse placement and treatment that is aimed at lessening his grave disability. He will be denied the right to refuse routine medical care which may be necessary and which is unrelated to his mental disorder." Something that makes me laugh, or rather shake my head, at the end of the report is that he is denied most of his rights, except for voting. And this is our government at its finest folks.

Dr. Ryfa submitted this evaluation to the Courts on February 2, 2015, some five months later. I am not quite clear from reading the records why it had taken so long to submit. It is stated there is a hearing scheduled for March 2, 2015.

Chapter Thirty-Five

Another hearing was held on November 18, 2014, and it was noted that "Defendant has dementia." Another evaluation was scheduled with Dr. Patricia Tyler, who was a Designee Medical Director of Napa hospital. This final evaluation determined, again, that Dennis had no chance of being able to testify on his behalf.

The report reported his current medications, as well as some questions as to whether or not he could make sound decisions regarding taking psychotropic medications. This one question was very interesting: "Does the patient present a danger to others if he or she is not treated with antipsychotic medication? Difficult to predict. He could without a known trigger or provocation." Too bad the doctors in the 1960s-1970s didn't opine the same way; otherwise he would still be rotting in jail, or dead due to his age before he killed his mother.

The doctor goes on to list a numerous of Dennis's deficits being, "Mr. Stanworth has a dementia marked by significant deficits in intellectual thinking, processing speed, memory, motor abilities and executive functions." The statement the doctor makes that can be used as an excuse to kill his mother was "These deficits were present at the time of the alleged crime and would have significantly impaired his decision making."

So, his mother suffered because he had strokes. I don't know; I have a hard time with that as a person who is not in the medical field. There are always excuses for why people act the way they do, whether it be their childhood or medically speaking. Once again, I believe people have a choice and he picked the wrong one. I wonder how his mother would have felt about all of this. Did his mom notice his decline, and if so, was she also making excuses? She tried her best to protect him in 1966 but it did not help. She stuck by his side, and this is how he repays her. Because he felt she lived long enough?

In the end, Dennis needed to be moved to another facility since he would not be restored to competency. The Public Guardian tried to place Dennis in another medical facility. They contacted thirty-three other medical facilities in the area and none of them would accept Dennis as a patient. I feel this was some sort of justice because he wouldn't be living out the rest of his life in a plush facility being taken care of. He would stay at Napa State Hospital to be taken care of until his last days.

Cecile took part in trying to take care of Dennis but where was Edmund? There is no mention of Edmund after this crime. Edmund passed away on March 16, 2015, at the age of eighty-four. At this time Dennis was seventy-three only eleven years younger, but Edmund was his adopted "father." On Edmund's death certificate it was noted that he had a master's degree and was a journalist for his usual occupation. He had lived in Solano County for twenty-five years, which goes back to when Dennis was paroled in 1990—very interesting. He moved out to California just for Dennis. His place of death was the UCSF Medical Center in San Francisco and cause of death was "Brain Herniation, Sub-arachnoid Hemorrhage, Cerebral Aneurysm Rupture." It noted that he had surgery on March 15, 2015, for external ventricular drain. He had an aneurysm burst in his brain and he passed away.

During this time Dennis was already diagnosed with dementia, so did he even understand that Edmund died? I almost feel like it would have been nice if he was aware; maybe that would have caused him the heartache he caused so many other families had by what he did to their loved ones. It sounds like I'm very revengeful, and in a way I am. Dennis never should have seen the light of day, ever. Our justice system, California in particular, has blood on their hands, Nellie's blood. Had he been kept in jail, she probably would have lived a longer life rather than it be taken from her.

Dennis's attorneys had requested that Dennis stay at the Napa Hospital instead of moving him to Solano County jail because of his deteriorating health and the jail could not provide the care Dennis needed. This request was granted so he was able to stay at the hospital.

They stated in their motion, "Moreover, because he is housed at Napa State Hospital, Mr. Stanworth's wife is able to supplement the care being provided by state hospital staff by visiting him daily, feeding, and providing a familiar loving face."

Dennis did not live much past this and passed away on April 21, 2015, roughly one month after Edmund passed. He had passed due to cardiac rest along with multiple organ failure. Cecile stood by his side all the way up to the end. She could have easily walked away and let him die, alone, in a hospital bed, but chose not to.

Cecile went on with her life. She was the executor of Edmund's estate, so she sold the house and moved to Fernley, Nevada, where her nephews lived. She must have loved her nephews because when she passed on April 28, 2017, she left her house to them. She died due to myasthenia gravis (which is a rare neuromuscular disease), pneumonia, and diabetes. The neuromuscular disease was the reason why she used medicinal marijuana. It is a very painful disease. She passed at the age of sixty-nine, two years after Dennis died. The only close family she had left was her sister who lived in North Cedar City, Utah. I reached out to her sister, but she has never responded.

The hardest part of this book was the fact that most people who were directly involved with Dennis are no longer alive. Most of my information came from court documents, transcripts, medical records, and speaking with relatives of the victims.

I was unable to find much information on Edmund, due to him being an only child and no other close relatives, other than Dennis.

There were quite a few people I contacted who did not respond, and I can understand that. I wanted their point of view and how they saw things and not just go by what Dennis said, but they lost that opportunity to set the record straight from their sides.

The reason I wrote this book was because the victims of Dennis were never recognized throughout the years. I have watched many true crime shows, have read numerous books as well as listened to podcasts, and this story has never been told. You have probably never heard of the "Linoleum Knife Rapist" until this book.

The other reason I was interested in this case was the so many injustices that happened. Granted some of these were in the 1970s, but Dennis's crimes should have carried more weight than his outstanding record in prison. Was Dennis talented and smart? Absolutely, but so are a lot of people in jail, and are still there.

One of the things that bothers me the most is there is no consideration for the victims or their families. The justice system has certainly come a long way since the 1970s, but how many cases do you hear of where the criminal is on death row for twenty years? Is that justice?

When you think of Dennis's last days on earth, do you feel sorry for him? To think of a loved one going through what he did you would tend to feel sympathetic for them. In this case, do you feel sympathy toward Dennis because how he ended up living his life at the end? That is a very hard thing to consider. Do you feel sympathy for a person who committed such heinous crimes, no matter how long ago it was? None of these women deserved what he did to them.

He stole the lives of two innocent young girls and betrayed the one person who stood by his side his entire life: his mother.

May they now rest in peace.

Epilogue

This case was very difficult to write about, not only because of the age of the case but also of the details of the crimes. I cannot imagine what Susan and Caree went through on their last day. I can only pray that they didn't feel any pain and died instantly. Caree may have held on, but she was in a coma and was not aware of what was going on. Nellie was hit from behind, so hopefully she didn't realize what hit her and the fact that her son was going to murder her. All of these scenarios are heartbreaking, to say the least. I will never forget these ladies and hope their lives will be remembered by others.

The one I need to thank for the most is God, for giving me the patience and perseverance to continue to write this.

My mother knew Caree when she was in junior high school, so that was my first connection to the passion I had for this case. I would like to thank Janet Hill; she was the lifeline for me to communicate with Susan's sisters, Verena and Carol, not to mention that she is a very sweet lady. Had it not been for Janet, I wouldn't have been able to finish this book with the information I had. Most thankfully is Verena and Carol, who let me into their personal lives so that I could learn about Susan and know her on a more personal level. I also want to thank the grandchild of Nellie for giving me their insight into Nellie's life and how she was a sweet grandmother who was betrayed by her own son.

Thank you to Cecile's nephews, Larry Collison's widow, one of the boys who found the girls (you know how you are)", and Mr. Michael Snedeker for their information and input.

I hope this book does justice for these ladies; they certainly didn't receive it in their lives on earth. God bless.

Photo of Susan Box Photo
Provided the Box Family

Photo of Susan-
Provided by the Box Family

Photo of Caree
San Francisco Examiner 8/13/1966

Short Stop Restaurant-2021

Caree's house-2021

Susan's house-2021

Dennis' house-2021

Dennis Stanworth
Sacramento Bee- 8/13/1966

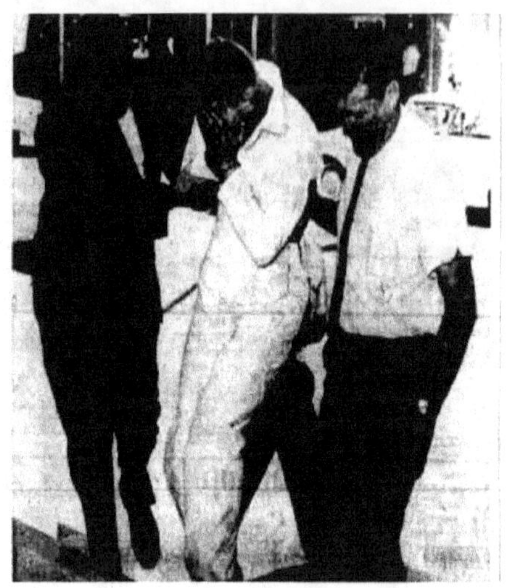

Oakland Tribune-8/19/1966

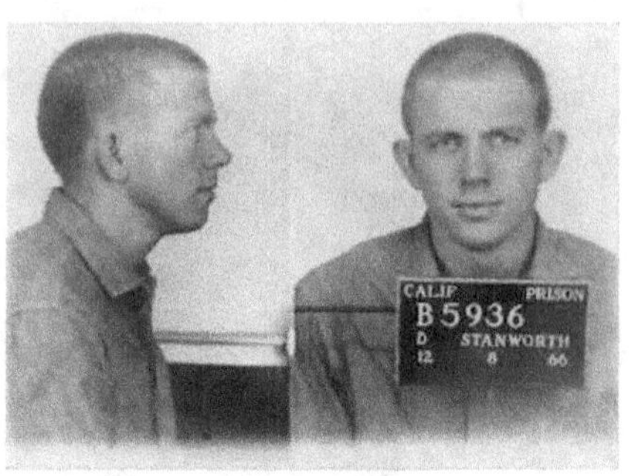

California Department of Corrections

Edmund Fink
Kansas City Star-March 29, 2015

Cecile Bonaudi Facebook page

Photo of Nellie, Thirl, Larry
Provided by Nellie's family

Photo of Thirl and Nellie
Provided by Nellie's family

The Citizen~1/13/2015